HOMO CATASTROPHICUS

Copyright 2024 © Louis Armand

This book is published under a CC BY-NC-SA 4.0 licence
https://creativecommons.org/licenses/by-nc-sa/4.0/

ISBN (print): 978-1-916541-07-8
ISBN (ebook): 978-1-916541-08-5

First edition.

All rights reserved.

First published in 2024 by Erratum Press
Sheffield, UK
www.erratumpress.com

Design and typesetting by Ansgar Allen

HOMO CATASTROPHICUS
The Revolt Against Civilisation

Louis Armand

ERRATUM PRESS
ACADEMIC DIVISION

We must, then, apply the principle of Doubt to Civilisation;
we must doubt its necessity, its excellence,
& its permanence.

– Charles Fourier, *The Social Destiny of Man:
Or, Theory of the Four Movements*

PREFACE	1
ALGORITHMIC STATE APPARATUS	3
"BARBARIC PEOPLES OF THE EARTH"	31
REALISM'S ANTIPODE	61
LITERATURE'S INCEST MACHINES	75
CONSPIRACIES OF NO FUTURE	91

PREFACE

Capitalism – the apotheosis, for Fukuyama & others, of what formerly, at least since the 16th century, was implied by the term civilisation – names that "event" in which crisis is institutionalised as the global protagonist *par excellence*. It stands at the end of a teleology spanning the history of statehood, writing & money. As Mirabeau famously wrote, "Not only the individual advances from infancy to manhood but the species itself from rudeness to civilisation."

Thus capitalism is civilisation in its ultimate phase.

Considered within the Judeo-Christian eschatology onto which Mirabeau's notion of social evolution is implicitly mapped, capitalism stands in direct relation not only to metaphoric "end of history" & "end of man," but to an Armageddon presaging the terminal shock of the literal "end of the world." The final ruin of a material *being* for the sake of an immaterial transcendental one, completes a movement within history of crisis conceived increasingly as neither contingency nor determinacy, but as an autonomous agent serving its own inscrutable ends.

This conception – cybernetic in character – is nevertheless recuperated for a (speculative, theoretical) humanism *after the fact*, a *posthumanism* that envisages itself as ostensibly living on, an avatar of self-witness beyond the extinction horizon, from which purview to critique or rectify, to re-evolve, within the technological movement of crisis itself.

The emergent "consciousness" of what has variously been called the Anthropocene, Entropocene, Capitalocene, stands in a curious relationship to that most fraught symbiote of capitalism, "the avantgarde" (whose appointed task was the *revolt against civilisation*). Where the avantgarde envisaged itself as revolutionary potential inserted *as if in advance* of historical forces, the posthuman evokes a recursive, strophic arrière-movement in which "the end" constantly self-supersedes.

Just as Lyotard construed postmodernism as modernism-in-a-perpetually-nascent-state, so the posthuman is the avantgarde at the end of history. We might call this Janus-like contiguity, *Homo catastrophicus*.[1]

Prague, August 2024

---

[1] See my discussion of Homo catastrophicus in the chapter entitled "Catastrophe Praxis," *Entropology* (Grand Rapids: Anti-Oedipus Press, 2023) 13.

ALGORITHMIC STATE APPARATUS

> Spectators are linked solely by their one-way relationship to the very centre that keeps them isolated from each other. The spectacle thus reunites the separated, but it reunites them only in their separateness.
> – Guy Debord, *The Society of the Spectacle*

With the advent of AI, theory finds itself at a crossroads, confronted by an "edge-of-the-construct," which has ceased merely to be a *metaphor* for the phantasmatic relationship between the technē of representation & posthumanist transcendentalism, rather it designates theory's own precarious situation, as *prosthesis of reason* & *autonomous critical agency*. This scenario, often depicted as a boundary between the human & the technological, reflects a preoccupation with simulationism & the control exerted by computational systems on "reality," as well as a desire to recuperate this "beyond of experience" for a new existentialism, a new humanism.

It's a readymade cliché that the emergence of Large Language Models necessitates a re-evaluation of preconceptions about intelligence, consciousness & the role of humans in a technologically constituted world, *et cetera*. Yet if the rapid development of AI & hyperautomation challenges both anthropocentric *as well as* post-Anthropocenic conceptions of agency, it does this not by indicating the rapid dis-integration of "subjective experience" within a "consensual hallucination," as William Gibson famously put it, of "reality" (modernism's hand-me-down), but by disintegrating the very framework of "experience" in general & of "consensus" in particular.

While terms like algorithmics & technicity are often affected to mean predetermined, end-orientated reductive systems that translate input into output, cause into effect, intention into action, their entire genealogy (from Aristotle to Mumford, Giedion, McLuhan & beyond) speaks to a poiēsis or *poetics* of spontaneity, indeterminacy, complexity. It isn't merely that algorithms are generative, but that they are *ambivalently* so. Every apparent algorithmic bias is *ambivalently determined*. This extends to the arbitrary, stochastic & interoperable nature of "representation," "experience" & "reality."

Drawing from Althusser's thesis on Ideological State Apparatuses, alongside Mark Fisher's capitalist realism, we may posit a subjective experience & consensual reality as emergent from – & as – *states of ambivalence*, such that the "concreteness" of social relations posited by (e.g. Marxist) critical theory is seen to be deeply intertwined with *ad hoc* algorithmic governance rather than actualising or reifying an underlying political teleology. Likewise the history of panopticism, simulationism & the "society of the spectacle" (as theorised by Bentham, Debord, Foucault & Baudrillard).

What is here called the Algorithmic State Apparatus transgresses *at every point* the logic of panoptic surveillance under conditions of AI – of subjective experience & the consensual-real – producing *human hypotheses* (radically simulacral egotic artefacts) from *solipsistic* neuro-computational networks (theoretical-real Universal Turing Machines). This *stateless* control system operates in the place where ideology cannot see – in the recursive hyperspace between omniscience & the unverifiable; necessity & the impossible – erecting edifices of pure metaphor, autopoetic & indeterminate, yet *as if* productive of all past, present & future realisms.

Edge-of-the-Construct

You're watching a film in which the protagonist is driving through a city, trying to escape, as if trapped inside a labyrinth. Eventually, after innumerable wrong turns & obstructions, they reach the proverbial end-of-the-road. The "city" ends precipitously & a starkly abstract Cartesian grid extends into infinite space. By now this scenario – & countless like it – has become the defining cliché of a whole genre of technosocial panic: the reification of an otherwise imaginary boundary between human & digital, as frontier myth of characters "trapped" inside a computer simulation. Such is the pervasiveness of this genre that students of Baudrillard like Achim Szepanski have been recently moved to assert that "the *goal* of every system or theory is to create a simulacrum of itself in space (other worlds) & in time (owner of the future)."[1]

But this scenario has long-ceased to be merely a work of science theory-fiction. On 17 January 2023, a *New York Times* headline read: "ARE WE LIVING IN A COMPUTER SIMULATION & CAN WE HACK IT?"[2] The idea that "the universe is a hologram, its margins lined with quantum codes that determine what is going on inside,"

---

[1] Achim Szepanski, *In the Delirium of the Simulation: Baudrillard Revisited* (Paris: Presses du reel, 2024) 23 – emphasis added.

[2] Dennis Overbye, "Are We Living in a Computer Simulation, and Can We Hack It?" *New York Times* (17.1.2023): https://www.nytimes.com/2023/01/17/science/cosmology-universe-programming.html

where the computational cosmic brane[3] takes over the role customarily reserved – in magic, superstition, organised religion & the myth of the state – for "higher powers," is hardly a novel idea. The distinction meant to be drawn from the *New York Times* article is that real science, not science fiction, is the domain (the "goal" according to Szepanski) of a cosmocapitalist algorithm. Moreover: that a contiguity exists between the causal determinism of cosmic supercomputers & a transcendental (financialised) cybernetics, an inflationary horizon across which homo catastrophicus universalises its "posthuman" destiny.

It seems that we are, as it were, on the cusp of a truly disturbing revelation, of which humanity – in a bizarre act of precognitive mimēsis – has until now played at being the author of.

Welcome to the "singularity."

On 30 November 2022, when OpenAI released GPT to the public, doomsday predictions about rampant antonymous AIs wreaking havoc across the world (& beyond), were already being offered as foregone conclusions. Yet the sudden advent of LLMs or Large Language Model AIs, of which GPT became the instant & ubiquitous representative, necessitated a radical reconsideration of what such foregone conclusions might actually mean.

It's by now a commonplace that the forms of hyperautomation which have rapidly co-evolved with LLMs pose consequences far beyond humanity's impending "extinction" at the hands of sentient machines (humanity appears to be accomplishing this end quite efficiently all by itself). Yet, it is no exaggeration to speak of an AI revolution, although it may be more correct to speak of a process occurring throughout the timeframe of the long Industrial Revolution, or what perhaps anomalously is still being referred to as the Anthropocene, Entropocene, or Capitalocene. If these terms deserve our interest, it is to the extent that they signal a deconstruction of humanist thought & the redistribution of its prerogatives (*consciousness*, *intelligence*, *subjectivity*), than the refurbishment of a genre of science fiction.

Already in the mid-twentieth century cyberneticians & quantum physicists had generalised the idea of information as a fundamental constituent of the universe: determinate of "reality" & not simply its

---

[3] The principal idea in brane cosmology is that the three-dimensional universe constitutes a brane inside a higher-dimensional space, sometimes referred to as "hyperspace." The suggestion, here, is that – based upon recent observations of existent cosmic megastructures – such a brane might be considered "intelligent," analogous to a "cortex."

descriptor, nor simply an artefact of its "effects." The emergence of LLMs ramifies a number of implications stemming from this – among them, the "meaning" not only of what universal general intelligence may be, but of what the exercise of power ultimately entails in relation to such an intelligence & *its possible operations.* The convergence of intelligence, power & language isn't a new topic (it's the subject of Plato's *Phaedrus*, c.370BC) – its manifestation as autonomous, hyperautomated technicity, however, is.

Mirrorworlds

In the expanded field of language, the question of intelligence is inseparable from the dynamics of signification – which is to say, the circulation & distribution of meaning, & thus power. Just as (for Derrida) every signified is always-already another signifier,[4] so too every dynamic relation is always-already an algorithm (a system of force-feedback or ramified bias), just as every data-node is always-already another calculus, *in advance of itself,* anticipating its own feedback. It's a dynamic evocative of Blakean possible worlds, of universes in grains of sand, coupled to a generalised "mirror dialectic" (Lacan) in which the simulacral "other" always-already sees "you" before you see "it." There's never a point at which a human protagonist stands in front of an empty mirror, waiting for its reflection to appear: before the protagonist ("the subject") even knows what it is, its reflection is *there*, in exquisite detail, *waiting to be recognised.* We might say, in effect, that it is the protagonist that is always somehow in process of *coming into view* within a scenery that not only perfectly anticipates it (the protagonist), but produces both its (the protagonist's) self-image & its perception of that image. If this "mirror dialectic" serves as a metaphor of an ideal artificial intelligence, this is because it assumes the form – not of a *reply* to the subject, but rather – of a *precognition.*

It's only possible to approach the Algorithmic State-Apparatus by understanding that this precognitive "effect" is a characteristic of that reality in which the subject-as-protagonist is *posited in the first place.*

---

[4] See Jacques Derrida, *De la grammatologie* (Paris: Éditions de Minuit, 1967) 88: "C'est que l'archi-écriture, mouvement de la différance, archi-synthèse irréductible, ouvrant à la fois, dans une seule et même possibilité, la temporalisation, le rapport à l'autre et le langage, ne peut pas, en tant que condition de tout système linguistique, faire partie du système linguistique lui-même, être située comme un objet dans son champ."

Something occurs within the very logic & structure of mimēsis that continues to attract resistance in the discourse around artificial intelligence & which recalls certain resistances both to deconstruction & quantum mechanics. The signifier (logos) does not *derive* from a socalled signified (eidos), it *produces* a signified – & *this* signified is never itself more than contingent upon the significations it in turn must perform (contingent, therefore, upon its own *possible future states*). Ad infinitum. For this reason, it isn't sufficient to envisage a simulacral "construct" emanating from some momentous artificial neural net, like a ghost or spirit, haunting or even *taking the place of* socalled reality – for the simple reason that this exquisitely detailed "construct," in order to not simply collapse in on its pseudo-autonomy, must be coterminous with the "apparatus" that produces it – the neural net – the signifying system – the mimetic economy – the mirror dialectic – the semiosphere – the "artificial intelligence," etc.

That is to say, it must be autopoetic, an algorithm of algorithms.

As a mode of signifying production inseparable from general conditions of signifiability (like a Universal Turing Machine at virtual lightspeed, into which every possible calculus is subsumed, as it were, as if "in advance"), the Algorithmic State Apparatus must not be confused with mere artefacts. We must be cautious of the way in which a hyperproduction of "exquisite detail" beguiles with a false opposition between two registers of mimēsis: one in the form of an inflationary ("substantive") realism & the other in the form of realism's "void." The first corresponds to a certain banality of gratified desire, the second to an anxiety expressed in its withdrawal. Or else the contrary: the second gratifying a revelatory desire – the end of the world, the void, nothingness – as the first proffers an anxious overabundance of possible worlds, endless novelty & limitless progress. But this instant resolution into the old binaries masks precisely those operations of mimēsis that only *appear to devolve upon them*, since they themselves are a product of the same aesthetic-ideological "apparatus."

Let's return to the opening scene: a city, a labyrinth, a protagonist trying to escape.

The edge-of-the-construct *as interrupted-line-of-flight:* from world-as-representation into metaphysical nonspace. Such is the narrative arc described in Daniel Francis Galouye's novel *Simulacron-3* (1964) & depicted in two film adaptations: Rainer Werner Fassbinder's *Welt am Draht* (1973) & Josef Rusnak's *The Thirteenth Floor* (1999). The revealed construct on the one hand – the world of signs, the prison-house of language, the reality pulled over our eyes – &, on the other, the Platonic-Cartesian armature on which it is built, of deterministic laws, of pure reason, of truth.

While presented as a topos of disillusionment, the meaning of this edge remains ambiguous, since it's unclear if it constitutes an "actual" void present within the construct "itself," or if it exists as the "signifier" of a void in place of an experiential reality available to the protagonist (who, like the totality of their environment, is also a "construct"). A simulacrum-within-a-simulacrum, in other words. An analogous moment occurs in the Wachowski's loose adaptation of William Gibson's Sprawl trilogy, *The Matrix* (1999; an eschatology of internecine (human-machine) war & the "redemption of man"), when the film's messiah-analogue, Neo, wakes from the immersive simulation (in which he has lived his entire preceding "life") into the "reality" of a machine dystopia, in which the meaning of that life has amounted to serving as nothing more than an energy-source (a literal duracell). Translate energy-source into data-source & the distinction between cine-fiction & contemporary "everyday life" grows perilous.

In any case, *The Matrix* – unlike *Simulacron-3* – maintains the possibility of an actual line-of-flight: not only an escape from the construct but the means to overcome it. The entire *Matrix* narrative represents something closely resembling the liberatory fantasy within which the protagonist of *Simulacron-3* remains immersed, in a *mise-en-abyme* from which there is, in fact, no exit. Yet the one is not simply a tragic view of the other: Baudrillard versus Debord, for example. There's more to it. It isn't, as Szepanski says (*à la* Baudrillard), that theory's goal – like that of capital in Debord – is to produce simulacra of itself at every point & call the sum of these an "image of reality"; rather, that theory – or something that calls itself theory – does so *unaware that it, too, is already a simulacrum*. Insofar as "theory" (or "capital") can be said to act *as if it were a subject*, then the point raised here needs to be understood strictly as stated: there is neither deception nor seduction at work on the level of this *non-awareness* – it isn't a strategy & its dimensions are unknowable. *The world pulled over your eyes*, as Morpheus says. Like the Freudian unconscious, this *non-awareness* has no being to which the simulacral can refer. In other words, the "goal" of such theory (capital) bears no relation to the operations constituting it: the algorithmic *as such* has neither object nor subject.

Dark Enlightenment

Consider another version of the same story: Alex Proyas's 1998 film, *Dark City*, which employs the conceit of an urban enclave shrouded in perpetual darkness. Here, each night on the stroke of midnight, as the inhabitants are put to sleep, the city physically rearranges itself, & the inhabitants' identities & memories are swapped around by secret agents (as in *The Matrix*, these *agents* are metaphors of the construct's "operating system," manifesting, at the level of the protagonist's "consciousness," in the antagonistic form of *secret agents* or *agencies* – which is to say, as classic *paranoiac "symptoms"*: the subsumption of the protagonist into this ego-construct thus takes the form of a dialectically-mediated narrative, in which the protagonist's heroic struggle against these agencies makes possible his own assumption of their role *under the fiction of autonomous action*). When the city "awakens," no-one seems any the wiser. This permutational construct – a seemingly monstrous, overly-determined logistic dedicated to maintaining a collective hallucination – presents itself as both *social* laboratory & Cartesian prison: an apparatus for entrapping – by way of a type of paranoiac-critical method – one particular individual's subjectivity, that of its "protagonist."

Indeed, the eponymous Dark City can be seen as manifesting an *algorithmic* function, inexorably corralling this protagonist into a confrontation with an "unavoidable truth." Like some Cartesian theatre, the city is both a "prison of the mind" & a metaphor for precarious dependence upon the "evidence of the senses." But at the moment when the protagonist confronts the city's secret agents, a dialectical movement is staged: the protagonist *becomes* the city & in doing so experiences the "reality" of their own "subjective fantasy." Which is to say, the "reality" of an individual who has become the undisputed author of their thoughts & actions.

In *Dark City*, the edge-of-the-construct trope is served by an impossible *topos*, Shell Beach, which the film's protagonists (in pursuit of some lost "memory") attempt to reach but which turns out to be a billboard advertisement stuck up on a wall on the fringes of the city. When the protagonists decide to "break through the wall," they find themselves on the precipice of outerspace. The edge-of-the-construct is represented here as a literal *shell*: the polis nested within a void (the analogue, but of a different rhetorical species, to Buckminster Fuller's "spaceship Earth"). Whether Cartesian grid or elaborate shell-game, this trope marks a crucial recursivity in the proposition of "the real": on the one hand, as that point at which the world is found to be missing; on the other, as that point at which it returns *in a vertigo of stark singularity*. Something like a dialectic of desire & (mis)identification is being played out here, reminiscent of both the primordial function of the Lacanian *lack* & Althusser's shadow beneath the lamp – & while it may present itself as an *ideological blindspot* (a point invisible to the subject because incomprehensible to it), it is just as much a point of *ideological fixation*, by which the socalled void *represents* an impossible desire (emancipation), which comes to stand for the impossible-as-such.

As Morpheus says to Neo in *The Matrix*: "Unfortunately, no one can be told what the Matrix is. You have to see it for yourself." This recalls an analogous scene in John Carpenter's *They Live* (1988) when the unnamed protagonist first puts on a pair of special sunglasses that allow him to see (as Žižek puts it) the secret world of ideological alienation & subliminal control *hidden in plain sight* all around. The edge of the construct can be anywhere – ultimately, however, it is always in some sense *within* the protagonist themselves – what Lacan calls the constitutive alienation of subjectivity.[5] In this way, the edge-of-the-construct presents itself as the ideal (dystopian) psychodrama, forming a rebus with the narrative of a hidden cosmic control system. The individual, under the burden of what has been revealed to them, is tasked with the work of emancipation while at the same time being confronted with the logical inference that any such emancipation may be no less a figment than the simulation from which they must escape. More, that the very revelation of being imprisoned may itself be the "masterstroke" of the simulation's design (that the world *is* a simulation now seems beyond doubt, it is the ultimate poisoned pawn, etc.).

This particular psychodrama arises precisely because the terms of the problem presented are those of reason itself: of logic & verification, of epistemology broadly speaking, of a forensics of "being." In each of the preceding scenarios, the edge-of-the-construct assumes a crucial function – not because it is framed by an arguable hypothesis – but because it is *represented* (right before our eyes) & "thus," in some way, *verifiable* (or at least *falsifiable*). Such a narrative proceeds on the assumption that such verification isn't itself already an effect of the construct, like the supposed

---

[5] In each of these is a re-staging of the Platonic "prison of representations," otherwise known as the analogy of the cave, the most enduring template of the "awakening to the world-as-simulation" theme: the archetypal blue pill / red pill. In this general scenario, a messenger appears bearing a hidden truth (or confirming a suspicion) & performs a *spectacle of verification*: revealing the machinery of the simulation & pointing to the existence of a hidden reality.

"internal contradictions" of capital (dialectically recuperated *for* capital when they aren't themselves artefacts of a dialectical "performance" of the contradiction or critique *of* capital, & so on). Yet this assumption is coloured with a certain amount of ambiguity, if not outright ambivalence: for Plato, the protagonist remains, in a sense, at the mercy of philosophical reason, to which they ultimately defer despite the evidence of their own senses. (In Plato, philosophy serves as the sole prosthesis of truth that isn't a mere mimēsis, yet it does so within a framework of allegory & metaphor constituted by Plato's texts.)

Just as science fiction exploits & produces an edge-of-the-construct for the purpose of dramatic ambiguity (as in Fassbinder's *Welt am Draht* – every world is a construct within another construct, which believes itself to be the "real" world [a version of the socalled Chinese box] – where exit, escape, transcendence are represented as narrative possibilities, but instantly foreclosed by the totalising incorporation of *all worlds* into a universal constructedness), so too "capitalist realism." This term, attributed to both Žižek & Fredric Jameson, & popularised by Mark Fisher,[6] denotes both the ideological character of all realisms & the specific nature of a reality arising from a critical *accumulation of capital* (pace Debord) as not only spectral or simulacral, but as omnipresent to such a degree as to have affected its own "foundation" of power. Yet this *accumulation* is, as Virilio rightly surmises (with Bentham clearly in view), simultaneously a *diffusion*. And it is by way of this apparently contradictory movement of the cumulative & the diffuse that the egoic concept of power (Plato's rational state) enters into a "state of emergency"[7] – which is also to say, a state of emergence. For Virilio, the diffusion of capital correlates to the *disappearance of politics* (the state) as such, or in Baudrillardian terms the disappearance of the political-real. "Capitalist realism," as the spectralisation of this emergent power, is given to imply both an omnipresence & omnipotence not only immune to contradiction or critique ("theory"), but in a sense precognisant of it (not merely "incorporating" contradiction – as per classical Marxism – but "producing" it *in advance* as an artefact of its own *autocritique*).

In this way, "capitalist realism" aligns with certain discourses on AI & machine sentience, & it shares with the notion of technological singularity the sense of a *point of no return*: a literal edge-of-the-construct that situates agency itself (everything from Platonic reason to the

---

[6] In *Capitalist Realism: Is There No Alternative?* (London: Zero Books, 2009).
[7] Paul Virilio, *Speed & Politics*, trans. Mark Polizotti (New York: semiotext(e), 1986) chapter 4.

Cartesian ego to the terminal fantasies of critical posthumanism) *beyond the possible*. Needless to say that in doing so it also broadly aligns with the history of cybernetics & poststructuralism, yet for Fisher there remains a tragic element (absent in Baudrillard) to the impossibility this absence of agency implies for not only bringing about but even *representing* an "end" of capitalist realism, since this very *act of representation* is made possible solely according to the specular logic of capital (Debord).

Above all, the meaning of the *impossible* vis-à-vis Fisher's omnipresence of capital does not correspond – contrary to Žižek's many insistences[8] – to what is reckoned to be *excluded* from representation, but rather to that which *pervades* representation &, like the panopticon, is everywhere "visible" yet nowhere "verifiable" (no act of reckoning, no measure of exclusion, can separate itself from it, let alone circumvent it).

In Platonic terms, the simulacral world of representations (mimēsis) isn't the anathema it appears, but – & this is the scandalous "secret" of all such metaphysics – is in fact the very technē of reason's power. This power is expressed, in *The Republic* & elsewhere, through the domination of mythos (of a fantastical – *poetic* – emancipation from universal law): the polis, like the eponymous Dark City – even in its struggle against the spectre of an oppressive supervening "reason" – remains stubbornly & insistently *subject* to reason's operations, even to the point of appearing irrational. Put otherwise, the very analytic which enables the overthrow of the clockwork "tyranny" of Dark City does nothing to negate this "reason": as with Landian accelerationism (& related posthumanisms indebted to Virilio, Deleuze & Latour), the insurgency of Dark City does not outstrip or transcend the operations of capitalist realism in any way, it merely inscribes another subroutine in its circuit of "production." More to the point, it does so by way of a neo-humanist fundamental fantasy: the attainment of the *impossible* by way of *living on* (that is to say, by inhabiting the zone *beyond the edge-of-the-construct*).

Traversing the Fantasy

When Jeremy Bentham proposed a radical thought experiment for the foundation of a utilitarian state, he did so in the form of a model penitentiary, which he named the panopticon: an all-seeing surveillance architecture that also served as a "psychocivilisational" machine (to borrow

---

[8] See e.g. Slavoj Žižek, *The Plague of Fantasies* (London: Verso, 1997).

José Delgado's terminology).⁹ The panopticon was designed to perform a dual analytic-synthetic function: to both individuate (by way of a specific regime of separation) & programme (by integrating "subjectivity" into a universal regime of production). The panopticon was intended to be no ordinary architecture, but a conceptual-logistical system (or ideology, not to be coy about it) – capable of manufacturing "consciousness": a prototypical artificial intelligence on the scale of the state, like α60 in Jean-Luc Godard's 1965 film *Alphaville*. Anticipating Darwin's & Freud's homeostatic notions of environmental "self-regulation," Bentham's panopticon points to a strictly "materialist" idea of consciousness & behaviour, mediated by way of "image technologies," like Orwell's Big Brother. Its mechanisms of surveillance are at the same time topoi of self-representation: a psychogeography of the Mind's Eye.

"It is obvious," wrote Bentham, "that, in all these instances, the more constantly the persons to be inspected are under the eyes of the persons who should inspect them, the more perfectly will the purpose X of the establishment have been attained." However, "Ideal perfection, if that were the object, would require that each person should actually be in that predicament, during every instant of time. This being impossible, the next thing to be wished for is, that, at every instant, seeing reason to believe as much, and not being able to satisfy himself to the contrary, he should conceive himself to be so."¹⁰

Panopticism thus operates on the basis of an asymmetry of *seeing-without-being-seen* (the inversion of the subjective illusion of seeing-oneself-seeing-oneself).¹¹ Its architecture is designed in such a way as to constitute the supervising awareness of this operation. It is nothing short of a kind of super-ego whose role is to implant itself in its subject & thus both modify & produce the subject's consciousness: what Žižek (echoing Lacan) calls *traversing the fantasy*. This fully-immersive, specular/cinematic architecture isn't inert; it is a dynamic system that comprehends & programmes individual & collective (social, political)

---

[9] José Delgado, *Physical Control of the Mind: Toward a Psychocivilized Society* (New York: Harper & Row, 1969).

[10] Jeremy Bentham, "Panopticon, or The Inspection House: Letter I," *The Panopticon Writings*, ed. Miran Bozovic (London: Verso, 1995) 29-95.

[11] Jacques Lacan, "The Eye & the Gaze," *The Four Fundamental Concepts of Psycho-Analysis*, trans. Alan Sheridan (New York: W.W. Norton & Company, Inc., 1981) 74. Cf Michel Foucault, "Panopticism," *Discipline & Punish: the Birth of the Prison*, trans. Alan Sheridan (New York: Pantheon Books, 1977) 195ff.

behaviour. And it establishes the paradigm that the individual *is an ideological complex within a system of power*.

As such, Panopticism needs to be understood as a general cybernetics.

The progress from a physical apparatus of subjection to a seemingly "immaterial" one of auto-suggestion – & by declension autopoēsis – was posited by Bentham to assume a certain immanence within a teleology of universal reason. In this, the panopticon *usurps* the very "nature" that it appears to *sublimate* into pure productivity, in order to construct a new programmatic mode of "naturalism" – or "capitalist realism" – & the seeming *self-evidence* of a world pre-ordained by the logic of industrial efficiency.

In this way the panopticon exposes a contradiction that stands at the heart of western individualism, which is that the individual so-conceived represents not the birth or rebirth of "humanism," but its end, as an artefact of the age of technological reproducibility – what William Blake called "the human abstract." In this, the panopticon could be viewed as a god-machine – & as "God is a sphere," according to Pascal (paraphrasing Hermes Trismegistus), "whose centre is everywhere & periphery nowhere," so the panopticon represents a universal decentring whose periphery is everywhere (the void of power). In place of the Cartesian obsession with "What gives consciousness its seeming primordial character?" there arises the prospect that not only is this primordiality an illusion, but that consciousness itself is "centred" elsewhere, in the diffuse architecture of the liminal-real. And if in Plato's cave "representation & truth" are asserted to comprise the founding authority of the state (of which the "individual – as in *Dark City* – is a metonym), then panopticism asserts – to the extent that it *asserts* anything – that representation corresponds to truth only insofar as it is a *mimēsis of power*. The power, that is, to *produce reality*.

Worldplay

On the unprovable assumption that whatever "produces" reality, "controls" reality... But what would it mean to "control reality"?

In general, what is awkwardly & erroneously called *commonsense* holds to the belief that certain things are self-evident & that this self-evidence is held in common. The fact that this is *not* the case has been the source of fundamental misunderstandings about the nature of social relations, among which the idea that the "individual" exists as a microcosm of "collective subjectivity."

As the Situationists deduced, the full implications of panopticism can't be grasped independently of a concept of *separation*. Bentham knew this: not only does the original penitentiary design (the "Inspection House" with which the panopticon was first identified) seek to isolate individual prisoners within their cells, but the cellular structure of the prison – as Foucault (ventriloquising Bentham) notes in *Discipline & Punish* – serves to *produce* the individual, as a reformed, prototypical social unit, destined for a new utilitarian (functionalist/rationalist) society. But the panopticon not only produces the separation-spectacle of social individuation, but universalises it as a *subjectivity-as-such*. This much Lacan had already derived from Marx, through the realisation that alienation doesn't *befall* the subject, but – insofar as there *is* a subject – alienation is *constitutive of it*.

Although Bentham didn't think in these terms, the distributed algorithmic system conceived in panopticism projects a movement of feedback that is constantly *dialectised*: the spectacle of productive alienation feeds into a radical negativity which it in turn sublates. For Lacan, this axiom informs the insistence that subjectivity *per se* can never be universalised as a "collective subjectivity," e.g. in the sense of Camus, for whom the *experience of alienation* represented the universal condition par excellence. There is essentially, for Lacan, *no social relation* – the constitutive alienation that produces the subject as "positive" feedback inscribes, at the level of social rapport, a "negative" feedback. It is for this that Lacan famously insists (elsewhere) that "il n'y a pas de rapport sexuel"[12] – for the straight-forward reason that there can be no alienational *capital* held in common: the alienation of capital rests in the experience of what Lacan calls *subversion* & which Rancière names *dissensus*.

In Debord's *Society of the Spectacle*, social control mechanisms are experienced in an evanescent way: the very "existence" of the spectacle (the production of real social relations) is deduced "paradoxically" from a general alienation-effect, held "in common," that separates the individual from everyday life. In the society of the algorithm, however, every experience is not only spectral, but pre-individuated: there is no alienation-in-general that can be held in common or aggregated into a "class consciousness" – each individual drifts through a "personalised" simulacrum of "everyday life." In this generative psychogeography no street is ever experienced *in common* by any two individuals & the Situationist

---

[12] Jacques Lacan, *On Feminine Sexuality the Limits of Love and Knowledge: The Seminar of Jacques Lacan, Book XX Encore*, ed. Jacques-Alain Miller (New York: Norton, 1998) 5n19.

dérive is itself détourned into a general alienism that cannot be verified simply by comparing accounts. Here, alienation is communicated as a mode of incipient paranoia where every point-of-comparison is "always-already" a coordinate in a seemingly infinite conversion programme.

The Algorithmic State Apparatus – a universal resource locator in this novel multiverse – projects each individual "enstatement" of everyday life as "unique" (& uniquely *real*). In the way a collapsed superposition is "unique" to those operations of observation that produce it, the Algorithmic State Apparatus works according to a system of ambivalences ramified into biases: perception itself produces an effect of *self-evidence*. These "parallel universes" aren't merely immersive subjective environments, they overlay the entire field of subjectivity & produce its signifiers, its realities. It isn't a question of two subjects ever being able to communicate their experiences to one another & in the process discover a regime of incommensurabilities – since all such communication (communication *as such*), *including* its incompatibilities, is always-already "subject to the algorithm." (It's not for nothing that the "reality principle" that emerges here resembles that of the paranoiac, for whom there can be no between-subjects but only the singularity of a persecution mania that, whenever it is perceptible *to others*, is viewed only as a mental illness.)

Yet this cannot simply be reduced to Goethe's proposition that "a person *hears only what they understand*."

It's "normal" for individuals to be in disagreement as to what constitutes their experience of reality – but disagreement about the "fact" of reality remains masked. The Algorithmic State Apparatus "masks" nothing: "reality" is indisputably *there*. No amount of subtle, persuasive or trenchant argument, no critical theory, disturbs its *fact*. Between the idea of a primordially experienced, antediluvian "realism" & the "hyperreality" of the most futuristic virtuality, there is no fundamental disagreement: all experience is equivalently real, even its unreality is real. The point simply is no longer that fine gradations of authenticity may distinguish one mode of being from another – the inauthentic from the authentic – the subversive from the collusive, etc., etc. What is called being *is, in its "total" genesis, algorithmic – within a recursive field to which there no "exterior."*

What is called intersubjectivity is like two particles in a state of quantum entanglement: observation of the state of one will automatically flip the observable state of the other. In Shakespeare, when Hamlet taunts Polonius by describing a cloud shaped like a whale or a weasel, something "beyond parody" intercedes in this game of signifying power – this *worldplay*. It isn't, of course, Hamlet's teasingly arbitrary likening of a cloud that concerns us: what is at stake is the agreement around there being a "cloud" in the first place – in other words, *that there is such a thing as agreement*. In effect, where Hamlet "sees" a weasel & Polonius "sees" a whale, the algorithm produces a metonymic equivalence: they both see a "cloud." This virtual "cloud" is the spectre of the algorithmic operation itself, in its seeming disembodied dimension, in which *everything is connected, everything is exchangeable* (from atom to cosmos, trope to schema… or from commodity fetish to Compaq's 1996 template for virtual distributed computing). Generalised into a system, the "cloud" is an evaporated, transcendental "capitalism," whose agency – the autonomous function Marx believed it had succeeded in universalising out of a base form of commodification (the fetish-thing) – is here subsumed into a radical ambivalence.

In Shakespeare, the weasel & the whale are what Marx called capitalism's "false choices." They float like synonyms on a linguistic-semantic surface of translation programmes, converters, filters that do not need to ramify an "agreed text" but instead produce situations in which a *mimēsis of agreement* can be "experienced." They hark to a kind of technological atavism of forms-without-content, archetypes capable in their universalism of activating & mirroring any desire whatsoever & thereby establishing a fundamental equivalence among them (including their "incompatibilities"), where "in reality" there is only what it is too tempting to call subjective fantasy – except that, this "fantasy" is, in each & every case, the very stuff of realism. It's for this reason that in *Hamlet* "the ghost" really is a figment, not because there is no such thing as ghosts (in the algorithmic state there are *only* ghosts), but because there's nothing its definite pronoun can index, nothing it can point at in a universe-in-common: "the ghost" is a superposition of all possible states of this spectre haunting Shakespeare's play – just as "the world," "the state," "the individual" are a seemingly infinite array of probabilistic phantoms in the datasphere (the proverbial "Cloud of Unknowing"[13]).

---

[13] Cf Vincent Mosco, *To the Cloud: Big Data in a Turbulent World* (Boulder: Paradigm, 2014).

The Algorithmic State is both Political & Ontological: Ontopolitical

Bias, as an inherent factor to any system, always implies a form of *governance*, & this is why logistics equates to both ideology & "something more" than ideology. As Aristotle says in the *Physics*, "It's absurd to suppose that purpose isn't present because we don't observe the agent deliberating." Totalisation, which is the *a priori* of ideology as such, evolves mechanisms of control – *even*, or *especially*, within those grey areas seemingly hostile or resistant to the observation of governance (areas of "chaos," "indeterminacy," "complexity"). The "problem" of *agreement* within the algorithmic state is not a point of vulnerability in the system, as Situationism would contend – as an opening, for example, of a movement of subversion, critique or détournement – but rather the genius of the system's dynamic. It isn't "error tolerant" but "error determined" – just as entropy, like Darwin's natural selection, isn't contingent to the system but its "determinant": *the self-evident truth that probable outcomes are probable*. When we speak of governance in terms of the algorithmic state, then, we need to understand it as not being a mechanism to incorporate contradictions – a characteristic attributed to socalled late capitalism – but one produced by contradiction & fed by it. If contradiction ordinarily corresponds to a positivist definition of "entropy," then we could say that the algorithmic state is an entropy machine driven to maximise its own condition, augmented (not subverted) by complexity, & so on. If it evades classical political-economic description, so too does it confound critique, not by some miraculous evanescence, but because it itself already produced those descriptions, those critiques.[14] If Lyotard spoke of postmodernism as modernism already in a nascent state, *post-modo*, then the algorithmic state "represents" a similar timetravel paradox.

Spectral accumulation, of such a degree as to collapse into a singularity, not only ruptures the illusion of teleology, historical materialism, linear causation, but the "time of capital" itself: the "present" of a certain mode-of-being. A spectre being that magical "thing," like language or the commodity, both dead & animate, an emanation of pure materiality that nevertheless demonstrates all the characteristics with which we imbue "agency": the condition of a "subject" that appears connected to

---

[14] As Johannes Birringer has also pointed out, for every descriptive system, "who or what is asking for this description?" *Theatre, Theory, Postmodernism* (Bloomington: Indiana University Press, 1991) 74.

its "subjectivity" only by means of a subtle thread of conjuration, fantasy or "psychic automatism" (reflex, mimicry).

"Commonsense" objections to the Algorithmic State Apparatus might begin by pointing out that the sheer logistical complexity of such a thing would render it impossible: as with Santa Claus, everyone would have to be in on the conspiracy. Yet the Algorithmic State Apparatus differs from its Althusserian forebears in a crucial respect: it does not represent a social control mechanism imposed by a conspiracy of power that seek to predetermine the mass of politically experienced reality. Instead, it "represents" – insofar as it represents anything – those mechanisms by means of which "reality" constitutes itself within any given observational framework, any point-of-view, any consciousness. These mechanisms are in a certain sense universal, but an aspect of this universality is that they always differ. That, irrespective, they present the appearance of aggregating into a more or less coherent & complete *system* indicates their extraordinary power to generate the phenomenon called reality.

That reality informs a common, shared experience isn't, however, the basis for generalisation it appears. Not only is such commonality a statistical artefact of the human sensorium & associated cognitive faculties, but the consistency of what falls within the meaning of both "reality" & "experience" is better defined by standard deviation than by a norm.

Reality Discriminators

On 27 February 2015, in a widely discussed post on BuzzFeed headed "What Colors Are This Dress?" Cates Holderness (@catesish) asked readers to vote on what colours they saw in the accompanying image of a striped dress: white & gold, or blue & black. "There's a lot of debate on Tumblr about this right now," Holderness wrote, "and we need to settle it. This is important because I think I'm going insane." The results of the poll – 2.5 million (67%) responded "white & gold," while 1.2 million (33%) responded "blue & black." #theDress itself was subsequently modelled at the annual Vision Sciences Society in Florida in June, where it was demonstrated that it was, in fact, blue & black: the conflicting responses were explained as being a product of aberrations in "colour constancy," where "different people's visual systems are assuming different lighting conditions, and therefore filtering differently, resulting in different percepts."[15] #theDress phenomenon highlighted a long-standing dilemma in the philosophy of perception, concerning the extent to which colour discrimination & object categorisation are objectively determined, to what extent are they universal, & to what extent are they subjective, language-determined or on a spectrum.

But if #theDress represented a statistically disturbing – if otherwise trivial – imbalance in the idea of a perceptible reality-in-common, more profound phenomena aren't in short supply in the fields of mental imaging, metacognitive awareness & the subjective experience of remembering.

Recently, an increasing number of studies have shown significant divergence in the way individuals process mental imagery & the capacity to do so. While some people can project vivid images in their "mind's eye" at will, others are congenitally unable to do so – one variant of a condition first described by the behavioural geneticist Francis Galton in 1880 but which has only recently been named: *aphantasia*.[16] In a pioneering statistical study, Galton sought to define "the different degrees of vividness with which different persons have the faculty of recalling familiar scenes under the form of mental pictures, and the peculiarities of the mental visions of different persons"[17] & to this end devised a survey concerning, among other things, the "illumination," "definition" & "colouring" of pictures that arose before the respondent's "mind's eye." The study & its results are described in an article entitled "Statistics of Mental Imagery," where Galton records the following:

> To my astonishment, I found that the great majority of the men of science to whom I first applied, protested that mental imagery was unknown to them, and they looked on me as fanciful and fantastic in supposing that the words "mental imagery" really expressed what I believed everybody supposed them to mean. They had no more notion of its true nature than a colour-blind man who has not discerned his defect has of the nature of colour.[18]

---

[15] Minjung Kim, "Highlights from the 2015 Meeting of the Vision Sciences Society": https://ecrcommunity.plos.org/2015/06/26/highlights-from-the-2015-meeting-of-the-vision-sciences-society/

[16] A. Zeman, M. Dewar & S. Della Sala, "Lives without Imagery: Congenital Aphantasia," *Cortex; A Journal Devoted to the Study of the Nervous System and Behaviour* 73 (December 2015): 378–380. See also further research by Nadine Dijkstra & Stephen M. Fleming, "Subjective Signal Strength Distinguishes Reality from Imagination," *Nature Communications* 14.1627 (2023): https://www.nature.com/articles/s41467-023-37322-1.

[17] Francis Galton, "Statistics of Mental Imagery," *Mind* 19 (July 1880) [301-318]: 301.

[18] Galton, "Statistics of Mental Imagery," 302.

Perhaps, to do justice, it might with equal validity be said there exists a portion of society whose volitional ability to "see things" warrants the name *fantasists* – or *hyperphantasics*. Galton's "men of science" may not have been in the majority, but that the great majority of those "men of science" selected to be his experimental subjects *were* aphantasics raises provocative questions about the relation between the scientific mindset – & the presumption of rationality – & socalled "mental imagery" (or a susceptibility to it). Questions that inevitably touch on Galton's own methodology & on scientific method in general, the capacity for abstraction or intellection, & so on. As one of Galton's respondents wrote,

> These questions presuppose assent to some sort of a proposition regarding the "mind's eye" and the "images" which it sees... This points to some initial fallacy... It is only by a figure of speech that I can describe my recollection of a scene as a "mental image" which I can "see" with my "mind's eye"... I do not see it... any more than a man sees the thousand lines of Sophocles which under due pressure he is ready to repeat. The memory possesses it, &c.[19]

Indeed, the question of this relation – between the scientific "mindset" & the tribe of fantasists – is raised by Galton himself, having noted that, "On the other hand, when I spoke to persons whom I met in general society, I found an entirely different disposition to prevail. Many men and a yet larger number of women, and many boys and girls, declared that they habitually saw mental imagery, and that it was perfectly distinct to them and full of colour..."[20] Two further "notable results" are subsequently drawn from the survey: "the one is the proved facility of obtaining statistical insight into the processes of other persons' minds; and the other is that scientific men as a class have feeble powers of visual representation" – leading Galton (whose own position is rendered somewhat ambiguous here) to conclude that "an over-readiness to perceive clear mental pictures is antagonistic to the acquirement of habits of highly generalised and abstract thought."[21]

The evolution of statistical method & clinical experimentation has since come to show that aphantasia is a heterogenous phenomenon with distinct aetiologies for each of its sub-types (such as individuals with selectively preserved mental imagery in a sensory mode – auditory for

---

[19] Galton, "Statistics of Mental Imagery," 302.
[20] Galton, "Statistics of Mental Imagery," 302.
[21] Galton, "Statistics of Mental Imagery," 303-4.

example – other than visuality [synaesthesia]). And while aphantasia has also come to be associated with an *impaired ability to recall the past & simulate the future*, the question remains as to the role of visual bias in the way "imagination" & the experience e.g. of temporality are represented or narrativised &, consequently, tested, & what conclusions are drawn even when self-reporting is augmented e.g. by testing cortical excitability in the primary visual cortex or the correlation between visual memory & metacognitive insight (or its lack) into its degree of precision. This isn't to cast doubt on the science, but to pose the question about how each of these "experiences" is *represented* & consequently *made to mean*. It is, in other words, a question about mimēsis.

Namely: is ideology a spectrum the way mental imagery is a spectrum?

Mind Blind

Althusser states at the beginning of his notes on ideological state apparatuses (1969) that:

> As Marx said, every child knows that a social formation which did not reproduce the conditions of production *at the same time as it produced* would not last a year. The ultimate condition of production is therefore the reproduction of the conditions of production.[22]

"What, then," he asks, "is *the reproduction of the conditions of production*?" Althusser's reply evokes the "tenacious obviousness" of the type of empirical self-evidence to which we have previously alluded but relates this to a novel problem: the relation of "everyday 'consciousness'" to the "*point of view of reproduction.*" And it is here, without concluding the transition this thought initiates, that Althusser points towards what we call the Algorithmic State Apparatus – not as an operation of the "state" or *polis* but as a phase or status, an "algorithmic state," in which this reproduction of the conditions of production obtains. It is worth considering this paragraph of Althusser's text in full:

> The tenacious obviousnesses (ideological obviousnesses of an empiricist type) of the point of view of production alone, or even of that of mere productive practice (itself abstract in relation to the process of production) are so integrated into our everyday "consciousness" that it is

---

[22] Louis Althusser, "Ideology & Ideological State Apparatuses: Notes towards an Investigation," *"Lenin and Philosophy" and Other Essays*, trans. Ben Brewster (London: Monthly Review Press, 1971) https://www.marxists.org/reference/archive/althusser/1970/ideology.htm – italics mine.

> extremely hard, not to say almost impossible, to raise oneself to the *point of view of reproduction*. Nevertheless, everything outside this point of view remains abstract (worse than one-sided: distorted) – even at the level of production, and, *a fortiori*, at that of mere practice. [23]

This topologically recursive movement stipulates *something like* an edge-of-the-construct phenomenon, whose movement of "recuperation" is fundamental to the production of consciousness in general & of subjectivity in particular. Beyond a simple staging of the Cartesian theatre of seeing-oneself-seeing-oneself – between the recuperation of the "real" as limit-experience & the internalisation of an "outside" as experience-of-the real – such a topology points to a force of "abstraction" that is holographic, complex & singular. The relation of part-to-whole – of individual to mass – is not that of a representation, simply, but of an inscription, such that the terms – part, whole – *do not precede* the relation that produces them (to paraphrase de Saussure). Moreover, this recursive movement of (re)production constitutes the relation itself: what Marx called real social relations are nothing if not the instantiation of this circulatory system *on which production is founded*.

It is in the "nature" of subjectivity that an idea of the *whole of reality* – which is to say, of *reality as whole* – is reproduced in subjective experience, & that the subjective point-of-view is ramified in the "point-of-view of reproduction" as the *point-of-view of reality itself.*

This is what we may call the holographic character of the abstraction to which Althusser alludes & in which the elusive (for Althusser) operations of the Algorithmic State Apparatus reside. The problem in Althusser's thought becomes clearer once we see that the edge-of-the-construct (or what Althusser calls "the metaphor of the edifice") isn't an artefact produced by a relation between "infrastructure" (base) & "superstructure" (state, ideology), it *produces that relation* & in doing so *produces its terms*. Such critical montage-effect obtains wherever dialectical thought advances its claims. Such thought is still active in Baudrillard's schema of the *disappearance of the outside* (what he calls "the real," as distinct from Lacan's usage) in the *precession of simulacra* (the hyperreal).[24] In the operations of the Algorithmic State Apparatus there is neither recuperation nor disappearance: no edge-of-the-construct ever obtains *in the first place* other than as a genre or trope in the production of discourse

---

[23] Althusser, "Ideology & Ideological State Apparatuses."
[24] Jean Baudrillard, *Simulacra & Simulation*, trans. Sheila Glaser (Ann Arbor, MI: University of Michigan Press, 1994).

(the discourse of experience; of the real, etc.). This trope – what both Lacan & Derrida envisaged as the "decentred" structurality of structure – isn't itself an edifice of any kind, it is rather a kind of ambivalence, a "tipping point" of signifiability or what we might call the between-of-metaphor, of one "structure" or another. It is, properly speaking, *algorithmic*, in the sense that it supports all possible configurations of bias, yet is irreducible to none.

If something like the neuro-physiological divergence of aphantasia can ultimately be said to affect *any* descriptive system (including, of a generalisable experience-of-the-real), then it would indeed be necessary to posit a bioinformatics that: 1. circumvents the recent turn towards a Gaia hypothesis (world as primordial meaning); 2. is irreducible to "embodiment" (aphantasia as techno-humanism); 3. remains unsusceptible to a therapeutics (isn't normalisable). Such an aphantasia – like indeterminacy, superposition & complexity – would not announce some kind of *perturbation in the real*; nor would it imply an "alternative" psycho-social norm where a universality of perturbative symptoms might indicate proximity to some *other*, hidden or occulted, real.

Consequently, insofar as it might be possible to speak at all, as Althusser does, of the "reproduction of the conditions of production," only in suspense of *its* unifying realism – of reproduction's *mimetic imperative* – could such an operation even begin to be "meaningful." In aphantasia, the problem of the "metaphor of the edifice" likewise subverts the opposition posed by Althusser between the two orders of enstatement: the "repressive state apparatus" & the "ideological state apparatus."

> As a first moment, it is clear that while there is one (Repressive) State Apparatus, there is a *plurality* of Ideological State Apparatuses. Even presupposing that it exists, the unity that constitutes this plurality of ISAs as a body is not immediately visible.
> As a second moment, it is clear that whereas the unified (Repressive) State Apparatus belongs entirely to the *public* domain, much the larger part of the Ideological State Apparatuses (in their apparent dispersion) are part, on the contrary, of the *private* domain. Churches, Parties, Trade Unions, families, some schools, most newspapers, cultural ventures, etc., etc., are private...
> What distinguishes the ISAs from the (Repressive) State Apparatus is the following basic difference: the Repressive State Apparatus functions "by violence," whereas the Ideological State Apparatuses *function "by ideology."* [25]

---

[25] Althusser, "Ideology & Ideological State Apparatuses."

The problem of "metaphor" here relates specifically to the assumption of ideology acting in a concerted manner upon an *experience-in-common* (whether, in fact, it pertains to "imaginary" or "real social relations").

Althusser's key insight, here, that the ISA functions *by ideology* – in other words, acting *in place of* coercive power, as a kind of prosthesis (repression by other means, or "soft" power) – anticipates Foucault's panopticism in which *"power" is omnipresent, a distributed ideological actor or signifying system, underwriting* all social relations or *meaning*. That Althusser's ISAs are – in contrast to the image of monolithic power – *pluralised* doesn't lessen the sense in which action is understood to be *aggregated*, on the one hand, & *directed*, on the other:

> If the ISAs 'function' massively and predominantly by ideology, what unifies their diversity is precisely this functioning, insofar as the ideology by which they function is always in fact unified, despite its diversity & its contradictions, *beneath the ruling ideology…*"[26]

Where the Repressive State Apparatus directs the ideology of the state at its subjects collectively (wherein the "individual" is only an instant of the collective), the ISA posits ideology itself as contiguous with the state as a whole (as "collective subject" reflecting the individual). The latter is a more or less sophisticated version of the crude antagonism represented by the former.

It is to this zone of antagonism *& its representations* to which the edge-of-the-construct properly belongs.

Ideology Accumulated to such a Degree it becomes its own Ghost

In the Algorithmic State Apparatus, antagonism manifests not at the level of representable power-relations, but as a generative procedure. Like the Generative Adversarial Networks (GANs) from which contemporary AIs have evolved, such "reality discriminators" produce the very possibility of representation (mimetic production) & thus of ideology. If the more subtly adversarial character of the ISA is precisely what, for Althusser, represent what is *at stake* in class struggle (because it escapes total control by a ruling class, so that the exploited classes can more readily express themselves through its contradictions), its unicity represents what remains "illusory" about the totalising narrative of this struggle.

[26] Althusser, "Ideology & Ideological State Apparatuses" – italics in the original.

For Marx the meaning of ideology is domination (domination of consciousness). Althusser reformulates this as three complementary theses (tracing an *ad hoc* dialectical movement anticipating Baudrillard's "four phases of the image"): 1. "Ideology is a 'Representation' of the Imaginary Relationship of Individuals to their Real Conditions of Existence"; 2. "Ideology has a material existence"; 3. "Ideology Interpellates Individuals as Subjects."[27] By substituting "image" for "ideology," Baudrillard arrives at the following:

1. It is the reflection of a basic reality.
2. It masks and perverts a basic reality.
3. It masks the absence of a basic reality.
4. It bears no relation to any reality whatever: it is its own pure simulacrum.[28]

In effect, this modulation from ideology-as-(agent-of)-representation, via ideology-as-(agent-of)-material-existence, to ideology-as-(agent-of)-interpellation-of-the-subject, describes a circulatory movement of "(re)production" that is itself produced algorithmically, as *its own (simulacral) subject*.

To speak of an Algorithmic State Apparatus, then, isn't to add just another term to Althusser's schema, since this schema – & the critique of ideology that continues to be explicitly or implicitly based in it (e.g. Srnicek's *Platform Capitalism* [2016], Wark's *Capital Is Dead: Is This Something Worse?* [2019]) – is, like the edge-of-the-construct, already an artefact of its own pseudo-objectification. Pseudo, because the edge-of-the-construct – or, the "outside" of ideology – is a mimetic figment, an "effect" of representation wherein the meaning of "experiential reality" is posited as exterior to itself. Pseudo, therefore, not *falsifiable* – since at no point is the edge-of-the-construct verifiable: like the shadow-puppeteers in Plato's analogy of the Cave, the edge-of-the-construct is a trope, a turning, fraught with ambivalence as to any given trajectory or itinerary or "content."

Althusser comes closest to this realisation when he writes that "the category of the subject is constitutive of all ideology, but at the same time and immediately I add that *the category of the subject is only constitutive of all ideology insofar as all ideology has the function (which defines it) of 'constituting' concrete individuals as subjects*. In the interaction of this double constitution exists the functioning of all ideology, ideology being nothing but its functioning in the material forms of existence of that

[27] Althusser, "Ideology & Ideological State Apparatuses."
[28] Baudrillard, *Simulacra and Simulation*, 7.

functioning."[29] Were this *nothing but* dialectical convolution, it would still indicate a region within Althusser's schema that might otherwise appear phantasmatic or even fetishistic: the autonomous or autopoetic character of these "turns."

Radical Ambivalence

At stake in the age-old dispute around mimēsis is not only the sufficiency of representation, but the suspicion that underlying it is something less than unambivalent. Just as the signifying relation defined by Saussure (sign-referent) is understood as *arbitrary*, so too representation (even, or especially, on a neurophysiological level) can't be understood as some kind of manifold in one-to-one correspondence with universally valid "concepts" or "real conditions" obtaining in "the world," but rather as a network of" (non)relations" whose underlying characteristic – that which permits it to operate – is indeed ambivalence. Moreover, the question of sufficiency has always been duplicitous, since – from its initial formulation in Plato's *Phaedrus* – it elides the subjection of *logos* to *eidos* (of representation to truth) with the potential autonomy of the *logos* (its capacity to act independently of *eidos*, in effect performing its own subjectivity).

The question about the "reproduction of the conditions of production" (as reproduction *of* capitalist reality) to which Althusser's thesis on the Ideological State Apparatus is the response, corresponds to the first "duplicity" of mimēsis – the second poses its own question, as to the status of reality *as* reproduction "itself" (objectless, autonomous, compulsive): "capital to such a degree of accumulation that it becomes an image," as Debord says.[30] As with Lacan's "dialectic of identification" & "dialectic of desire" (to which Althusser's theory of the ideological subject is indebted), such a movement ramifies – rather than merely repeats – the phantasmatic character of (the capitalist subject's) "real experience." Mindful that the category of the subject, in Althusser, is bound to the assumption of a "point-of-view" (that of reproduction itself) just as, in Lacan, it is bound to *the assumption of an "image."*

To the extent that we might speak of an aphantasia of such an *assumption*, it's necessary to consider that – in the first place – "reproduction

---

[29] Althusser, "Ideology & Ideological State Apparatuses."
[30] Guy Debord, *The Society of the Spectacle*, trans. Donald Nicholson-Smith (New York: Zone Books, 1995) §34.

of the conditions of production" implies not a critical-mass accumulation of capital, but of the circulatory effect that sustains & valorises it: the *reproduction of difference*.[31] To invert the usual Situationist formula, "the spectacle" – as capital accumulated to such a degree it becomes an image – emerges precisely to the extent that capital accumulation is détourned. However paradoxical it may seem, the ideological force of capital is entirely dependent upon the *interpellation of difference* & not the contrary. And this difference is marked, above all else, by an ambivalence to the terms it causes to be brought *into relation* or into *discrimination*.

This, then, is the unacknowledged meaning of "subject" in Althusser's thesis. And it is as a locus of difference that this subjectivity connotes an "algorithmic state" (as a system of ambivalences that nonetheless ramify).

At issue, here, is not the usefulness of a given "technology" in elaborating a thought experiment in social engineering, but a technicity of the subject on the basis of which any *prosthesis of experience* would be possible in the first place & between which something like a correspondence might evolve to the point of a mirroring or "dialectic of identification." If the promise of industrialisation – that through emancipation from onerous labour & the bondage of a feudal-mercantile system – was to produce the "individual" as paradigm of autonomous social agency, this production has from the outset been accompanied by a doppelganger, which in turn has dreamt of becoming an auto-mobile self-regulating entity within a distributed field of technological possibility.

When in 1791 Bentham advanced his prototype *social control media*, few may have imagined it signalled the instigation of a cybernetic revolution (long forecast, at least since Plato's analogy of the cave) which would eventually arrive – by way of Babbage's analytic engine, Tesla's thought camera, Delgado's stimoceiver, Turing's electronic brain, Canova's smartphone, BrainGate, Neuralink & the phenomenon of generative AI – at an algorthmic state apparatus that would not simply affect a passable mimēsis of "thought," human or otherwise (thus merely extending the classical allegory of Xeuxis & Parrhasios), but for all intents & purposes be indistinguishable from it. That the metaphorical edifice of Bentham's analytic architecture for social reprogramming could have thus evolved, by diverse means, into the hyperconnected dataverse of

---

[31] Or what Derrida calls *différance (*differing-deferral). See Jacques Derrida, "Différance," *Margins of Philosophy*, trans. Alan Bass (Chicago: University of Chicago Press, 1982) 3-27; also Jacques Derrida, "Cogito & the History of Madness," *Writing and Difference*, trans. Alan Bass (Chicago: Routledge, 1978) 31-63.

mobile "smart" devices, the "internet of things," & the quasi-infinite, exquisitely detailed, virtually instantaneous monadologies dreamt by an already multi-generational cascade of LLMs, should perhaps come as no real surprise.

The live interface that GPT & its analogues today provide for millions of "users" globally – generating unique, instantaneous & varyingly complex interactions for each of them – may nevertheless still represent what, in Derridian parlance, amounts to a "prehistoric child's toy": yet this should not detract from the sheer force of the mimetic revolution that propels this dawning cognisance. Just as Bentham envisaged a rational surveillance state *without need of an overseer* (a real system of distributed power vested in imaginary &/or symbolic relations), so the dialectic of reason itself – historically besotted with its "reflections" – has devolved into an entity of inscrutably stochastic operations & cosmically-proportioned reservoirs of data as disproportionate to the singular, contemplative ego contrived by Descartes as might be imaginable.

If the algorithmic state is an instantiation of this "fact," then the cyber-political reality to which it "gives rise" must be no less nuanced & differentiated than it is. Monolithic power has always been a kind of travesty, just as its critique is a kind of travesty, a pas-de-deux in the Cartesian theatre for an audience of convex mirrors.

"BARBARIC PEOPLES OF THE EARTH"

> The long, dark night of the end of history has to be grasped as an enormous opportunity. The very oppressive pervasiveness of capitalist realism means that even glimmers of alternative political & economic possibilities can have a disproportionately great effect. The tiniest event can tear a hole in the grey curtain of reaction which has marked the horizons of possibility under capitalist realism. From a situation in which nothing can happen, suddenly anything is possible again.
> – Mark Fisher, *Capitalist Realism*

Any art that co-operates with the prevailing ideological structure of power can be subsumed under an "aesthetics."[1] On this principle, the association of the avantgarde throughout its history with a generalised *anti-aesthetic* bears within it broadly political connotations of economic & class antagonism, traceable to its origins in the militant revolutionary discourses of the nineteenth century across the political spectrum. Yet the notion of a specifically proletarian or working-class avantgarde is rife with paradox – stemming firstly from the fact that, historically, it has been the avowed function of the avantgarde to affect revolutionary *class consciousness* in the first place, & secondly from the necessity to contest precisely those ideological forces seeking to legislate the meaning of *work* & its role in political ontology.

Though having evolved in direct symbiosis with market capitalism, the avantgarde – in its militant, anti-institutional phase – emerges from an adversarial stance towards the "abstraction" & "impoverishment" of labour in the production of cultural surplus-value. In refusing the industrial work ethic as alienated & dehumanising – & *l'art-pour-l'art-isme* as its mystification – this emergence (from Blanqui & Bakunin to the Situationists & Arte Povera) manifests as a form of radical counter-work, one which sought to circumvent what Nick Land has called "the rage of jealous time" & "matter's positive effacement by utilitarian society."[2] In doing so it salvages notions of *usedness* & *uselessness* (as

---

[1] For a detailed examination of the question of "aesthetics," see David Vichnar & Louis Armand, "Aisthēsis & Literature," *Oxford Research Encyclopaedia of Literature* (Oxford: Oxford University Press, 2017): https://oxfordre.com/literature/view/10.1093/acrefore/9780190201098.001.0001/acrefore-9780190201098-e-104

[2] Nick Land, *The Thirst for Annihilation: Georges Bataille & Virulent Nihilism* (London: Routledge, 1992) 65.

determined by the capitalist work ethic), & *entropy* (as later delineated in cybernetics), for a critical affirmation of the art (or anti-art) of everyday life. Land draws on Georges Bataille's concept of general economy & "expenditure without reserve"[3] to posit such a counter-work in a virulently antagonistic relation to the logic of surplus production. "Expenditure without reserve" opens within cultural labour the space of an ecstatic chthonic function, through the purging of normative social desire. This radical potential can be understood as the means of avantgarde art to affect contradictions in the instrumentality of Power (capital), in such a way that Power itself (in its mechanism of desiring-production) is caused to dissipate in a histrionic effort to re-normalise & re-commodify.

Redolent of a negentropic movement, exceeding the ends assigned to it by its socially "productive" function, the avantgarde's convulsive re-potentiating of everyday life stands as remote from capitalism's commodification of existence as it does from Gautier's notorious pronouncement that

> il n'y a de vraiment beau que ce qui ne peut server à rien; tout ce qui est utile est laid, car c'est l'expression de quelque besoin, et ceux de l'homme sont ignoble et doûtant, comme sa *pauvre* et *infirme* nature.[4]

While Marx argued that the first condition of art is that it is not commerce, nor is art a reason of State: the socially-transformative programme of the avantgarde had thus to be situated in an antagonistic relationship to *servility in general*, & not in the trivial opposition of aestheticism & utility, or a *technē politikē*. Breton & Trotsky make this the main polemical thrust of their anti-Stalinist manifesto, "Towards a Free Revolutionary Art," written in Mexico City in 1938. In it they argue that "the imagination must escape from all constraint & must, under no pretext, allow itself to be placed under bonds." While "True art, which is not content to play variations on readymade models but rather insists on expressing the inner needs of mankind in its time –

---

[3] Georges Bataille, *The Accursed Share*, vol. 1, trans. Robert Hurley (New York: Zone, 1991) 21ff.
[4] Théophile Gautier, *Mademoiselle de Maupin* (Paris: Charpentier, 1880) 22: "true beauty resides only in that which can serve no purpose: all that is useful is ugly, for it is the expression of some need, & those of man are ignoble & disgusting, like his *impoverished & infirm* nature." [Translation mine – emphasis added.]

true art is unable not to be revolutionary; not to aspire to a complete & radical reconstruction of society."[5]

In what can be read as a call for renewal of the avantgarde's revolutionary project – after WW2, the "failure" of 1968, & the "triumph" of neoliberalism during the period since – Mark Fisher, in his 2009 collection of essays, *Capitalist Realism*, argues that, "If neoliberalism triumphed by incorporating the desires of the post 68 working class, a new left could begin by building on the desires which neoliberalism has generated but which it has been unable to satisfy"[6]; just as the historical avantgarde (culminating in Surrealism) had emerged from the foreclosure of those mass emancipatory desires aroused in the democratic revolutions of 1848 & which the triumph of the bourgeoisie was incapable of satisfying. "What is needed," Fisher insists, "is a new struggle over work & who controls it" – to which we might add, *a new struggle over the concept of the "working class"* & the ideology of *work* that defines *it*.[7] For in the proposition of an aesthetic economy of counter-work there is also a proposition for a counter-politics of social relations & the corporate ontology that has continued to underwrite them.

Work as Critical Self-Consciousness

With the appearance of Vorticism in 1914, the formation of the post-WW2 Independent Group, & the public confrontation between cybernetics & auto-destructive art in the form of the Destruction in Art Symposium of 1967 & the Cybernetic Serendipity exhibit at the ICA in 1968, lineaments of a working-class avantgardism come into view that define a major polemical axis in modernist & contemporary "British" art. Constellated around figures like Henri Gaudier-Brzeska, Eduardo Paolozzi & Gustav Metzger, this axis represents more than a series of historical contingencies. At its core lies a radical reformulation of the concepts of "work" & "class" drawn directly from the circumstances of a revolutionary art, its practice & its methodology. Elements of this development may be seen as describing a synthesis (bastardisation) of Cubo-Futurism, Dada, Surrealism & the Situationist tendency, in disputation with that return to critical purism that culminates in

---

[5] André Breton & Leon Trotsky [originally signed André Breton & Diego Rivera], "Manifesto: Towards a Free Revolutionary Art" (1938): www.generation-online.org/c/fcsurrealism1.htm

[6] Fisher, *Capitalist Realism*, 79.

[7] Fisher, *Capitalist Realism*, 79.

Peter Bürger's revisionist dissertation, *Theory of the Avantgarde* – a text designed as much to declare an end of the avantgarde as to 'theorise' it. Whatever may be said concerning the ambivalence of Bürger's text in those polemics around the socalled postmodern turn in art during the 1970s,[8] what commands our attention in the line of aesthetic inquiry running from Gaudier to Paolozzi & Metzger is how this ambivalence is ultimately rooted in a conception of 'work' that continues to mystify critical theories of art history. And just as the reach of Bürger's argument has been *de facto* extended via the counter-revisionism of Rosalind Kraus, Hal Foster, Benjamin Buchloh & Yve-Alain Bois (see *Art Since 1900*), so it, too, requires renewed critique.

Halfway through *Theory of the Avantgarde*, Bürger advances what will be a recurring thesis, that – in its historical formulation – the avantgarde had always viewed the dissociation of art "from the praxis of life" as art's dominant characteristic in bourgeois society.[9] Bürger argues that "One of the reasons this dissociation was possible is that aestheticism had made the element that defines art as an institution the essential *content* of works" – a coincidence that was above all necessary, in Bürger's estimation, "to make it logically possible for the avantgarde to call art into question."[10] Two factors need to be immediately addressed here. The first is the somewhat circular argument that emerges around this self-reflexivity of "content," wherein an emergent critical self-consciousness of art is simultaneously bound to self-supersession & obsolescence, since the "element that defines art" can in this relation be one only of anachrony to an art (or technē in general) that *calls itself into question*. The second is the confusion of aestheticism, as a *determining logic* of the meaning of art in "bourgeois" society, with the *abstractive logic* of the commodity in general, which should be identified as the real determining force here. Aestheticism is in effect nothing but a mystification of (sovereign) power, while the question of the institutionality of art (& of aesthetics in general) is directly bound to the question of power itself, whose signifying force – in industrial society – is communicated via the medium of commodification (its ideological social "content," in effect,

---

[8] See *The Anti-Aesthetic: Essays in Post-Modern Culture*, ed. Hal Foster (New York: The New Press, 1983).

[9] Peter Bürger, *Theory of the Avant-Garde*, trans. Michael Shaw (Minneapolis: University of Minnesota Press, 1984) 49.

[10] Bürger, *Theory of the Avant-Garde*, 49 – emphasis added.

substituting as a *technē* of experience, of "consumption"). It is, in short, the relationship of metaphysics to technology.

These factors intersect in what has become a quite conventional dialectical reading of the avantgarde, in which a certain false opposition is established between aestheticism's rejection of "means-ends rationality" & the historical avantgarde's "attempt to organise a new life praxis from a basis in art."[11] Yet far from the one negating the conditions of the other, we can see that both are complementary aspects of the same critical impulse & informed by the same abstractive logic. Yet it is only in its most Stalinist manifestations that anything which Bürger might be able to call "the historical avantgarde movement" here – that is, in its most reactionary appropriation – can be described as attempting "to do away with the distance between art & life" & to characterise this as still having "all the pathos of historical progressiveness on its side"[12] (as if the organisation of "a new life praxis" & the critique of "bourgeois society" amounted to nothing but a crude revisionism, through which the dichotomy "art & life" remains nevertheless preserved & fixed in its meaning). It is not for nothing that this tendency is precisely what Adorno & Horkheimer identify with the operations of a culture industry[13] – in which, as Bürger says, the institutionalisation of the avantgarde "has brought about the *false* elimination of the distance between art & life."[14]

Unstated in this equation is the question of work.[15]

Just as Bürger confuses the organisation of a new "life praxis" with "historical progress," so too he fixes the conception of *work* within precisely that framework of means-ends rationality against which both aestheticism & the avantgarde define themselves. Consequently, in addressing the avowed anti-art of what he terms "Dada manifestations," for example, the most he is able to do is argue that it "does not have the character of work" – whereas the contrary needs to be grasped in order to understand how the work paradigm (along with the relation between the *ideology of work* & the category of the *work of art*) is itself deconstructed by the nascent cyberneticism of the avantgarde. In this regard, also, it is necessary to examine the movement, built into Bürger's schematic, from

---

[11] Bürger, *Theory of the Avant-Garde*, 49.
[12] Bürger, *Theory of the Avant-Garde*, 50.
[13] Theodor W. Adorno & Max Horkheimer, "The Culture Industry: Enlightenment as Mass Deception," *Dialectic of Enlightenment*, trans. John Cumming (London: Verso, 1979 [1944]) 120-167.
[14] Bürger, *Theory of the Avant-Garde*, 50 – emphasis added.
[15] And, by implication, of a certain *false* (aesthetic) labour.

the "dignifying" of art-work as anti-labour, to its "impoverishment" as institutional labour. The otherwise unacknowledged relationship between the "dissociation of art & life" – as the context of the "aestheticist work of art" – & the impoverishment of labour under the social provisions of industrial capitalism, underpins a further misconception about the *constitutive* alienation of capitalist subjectivity (articulated through the abstraction of labour),[16] of which the "autonomy" of the avantgarde (vis-à-vis the "alienation" of art-work) is in effect the critical consciousness.[17]

It is here that the significance of Bataille's re-reading of Marx & Hegel must come to bear upon the idea of the avantgarde, as a "mode of production" of dissipative structures, in which "production" is itself understood as a *means of expenditure*.

For Bataille, dissipation & expenditure are not the (negative) consequences of a withering or impoverishment of (aesthetic) labour, but its *raison d'être*. And not only its "reason" but in fact its condition. As Derrida has noted, if "work" for Bataille is the discourse of reason itself (as Bürger tacitly assumes), it is no less the case that in its generalisation as the *ideology of labour* – enlarged to "include within itself, & anticipate all the forms of its beyond, all the forms & resources of its exterior… in order to keep these forms & resources close to itself *by simply taking hold of their enunciation*"[18] – it necessarily evokes a certain anti-work which, while appearing to be already comprehended by it, nevertheless threatens to exhaust (impoverish) the discourse of work itself. It does this, moreover, not by *opposing* an idea of alienated labour, but by inscribing, in the same language as this alienation, that which "exceeds the opposition of concepts governed by its logic."[19]

It is in this that Bataille situates the real deconstructive potential of this avantgarde (entirely opaque to Bürger's rationale), which does not resolve itself by a simple dialectical gesture of negation, since its

---

[16] Karl Marx, *Outlines of the Critique of Political Economy*, trans. Martin Nicolaus (London: Penguin, 1973) 693.

[17] Arnold Hauser offers an important distinction between the autonomy of art & the economic (in)dependence of the artist, noting that "it was only romanticism's bad conscience that attached such extraordinary value" to the semblance of this division-of-labour, informed by an "inhibited attitude toward everything *material & practical*, not the fact that he plies his art for a trade." Arnold Hauser, *The Philosophy of Art History* (Evanston: Northwestern University Press, 1985 [1958]) 337.

[18] Jacques Derrida, "From Restricted to General Economy: A Hegelianism without Reserve," *Writing & Difference*, trans. Alan Bass (London: Routledge, 1978) 252.

[19] Derrida, "From Restricted to General Economy," 252.

movement is one of an *excess* that is both "necessary & impossible," whose effects – as Derrida says – "fold discourse into strange shapes"[20] that, verging upon the *formless*, defy recuperation either for an instrumentalist system of value-production or its aesthetic contemplation. The logic of work as dissipation (entropy), & consequently the reconceptualising of modes of production as modes of expenditure, requires a re-examination of the framing of the aesthetic problem as it stands in the work of Bürger & his critics, if only to emphasise what is most radical in this movement.

Alienation(ism) & the Avantgarde

Bürger's complaint about the exhaustion of the historical avantgarde in its institutional iteration stems in no small measure from a perception of the neo-avantgarde's incapacity to produce a *shock value* that is historically necessary rather than merely faddish.[21] It suggests that art-work needs to be distinguished from an auratic, ritual phase – in Walter Benjamin's terms – as much as from a commodity phase, whose relation to the "new" is one of a mechanical & otherwise arbitrary reflex. In either case, the distinction rests on an appreciation of the capacity of the *artwork* – & only indirectly the *aesthetic labour* of the artist – to produce not only an effect, but a relation to "historical necessity."

Such "reified monuments"[22] of aestheticised labour distort a socio-economic relation into a teleology of the order of an historical materialism. In thus denying the abstract arbitrariness of the artwork as *surplus-value*, Bürger remains blind to the standard of auratic kitsch to which avantgarde labour is thereby to be held – as a category of production apparently transcending the constitutive alienation of work in general (that is to say, as a *class*). Likewise the standard of historical necessity does no more than mystify that *ideological social content* which is the supposed measure of art's capacity to shock. Yet what of an art *work* that fails to reify in this way? That fails, so to speak, to correspond – like Nietzsche's laughter – either to some dour fatalistic teleology or to the entropic effluvium of a culture industry driven by rampant inflation, producing neither aesthetic

---

[20] Derrida, "From Restricted to General Economy," 253.
[21] Bürger, *Theory of the Avant-Garde*, 50.
[22] This is an expression developed by Frederic Jameson in his essay "Postmodernism & Consumer Society," *The Anti-Aesthetic: Essays on Postmodern Culture*, ed. Hal Foster (New York: The New Press, 1983) 113.

value of "shock" nor its commodification (as if these weren't already the same thing)?

In the age of Taylorist scientific management, on course for what Harvey Wheeler in 1968 would call the Cybernetic Revolution,[23] the easy dichotomy between aesthetic non-work & means-ends rationalism is complexified in numerous & subtle ways. Simple binary antagonisms, of the quasi-Hegelian kind favoured by Bürger, had already begun to give way to increasingly logistical structures as the paradigm of a revolutionary movement. Concepts like that of distributed power, advanced by the utilitarianist Jeremy Bentham, devolved by turn into a general thinking about autonomous systems, like Darwinian evolution, the Freudian unconscious & quantum physics, in which indeterminacy vied with causality as the motive principle. While thermodynamics & mechanical computing likewise provided the underpinning logics of industrial modernity – regardless of all the avowals of historical necessity, manifest destiny, or the perfectability of Man that sought to extract ideological validity on modernity's behalf – they also brought into view forces equally capable of disrupting the existing socio-economic (as well as aesthetic) categories & of negating the very idea of progress itself. And by consequence, any linear schematisation of an avantgarde.

In this conjunction of complexity & abstraction, we see that "the pathos of historical progressiveness" that supposedly haunts the recursions of the avantgarde is that of Bürger's schematisation itself.

It's not enough to acclaim a certain machine aesthetics or proletarianisation of modernist art, as the terrain for marking out a conception of aesthetic labour within a larger revolutionary discourse – as if the movement of the avantgarde were simply a mirror held up to the "innovations" of the industrial sector (in the false belief, among others, that there are, indeed, independent sectors, or that the institution of art itself – & society *itself* – is not *integral* to the operations of modernity as a whole). The question is rather how the avantgarde articulates (produces) this critical logic in the *failure* of "historically necessary" production, or non-production. Not as the conservation of a revolutionary style, genre or *sense of moment* (the "shock of the new"), but as a general movement of a *destabilisation of frameworks*.

It is a widely repeated truism that Britain – "birthplace" of the Industrial Revolution – lacked a comparably radical aesthetic movement

---

[23] Harvey Wheeler, *Democracy in a Revolutionary Era* (Santa Barbara: The Centre for the Study of Democratic Institutions, 1968) 14.

in response to it, as if the socio-political fact of advanced industrialisation had obviated the need for an avantgarde – just as, though home to Marx's researches on Capital, it somehow obviated the need for a "worker revolution." In the face of such complacent self-evidence, it is necessary to point out that the absence of an avantgarde in Britain is a myth & yet this myth has gone some way in precluding the institutionalisation of otherwise isolated aesthetic tendencies construed as little more than footnotes to art history.[24] Such is, to a greater or less extent, the case with Gaudier, Paolozzi & Metzger who – along with David Bomberg, Jacob Epstein, James Fitton & the Alpha Group, & Richard Hamilton, among others – have conventionally been cast in the role of local adjuncts to the more consequential (& thus more vigorously commodified) tendencies of Futurism, Pop Art & Conceptualism.

More than a conspicuous marginalism links these artists. Metzger had met Paolozzi, along with another member of the Independent Group, Nigel Henderson, in 1944, & later enrolled in Bomberg's painting & composition class at the London Borough Polytechnic in 1946. Bomberg had, with Gaudier, been a sometime fellow-traveller of Vorticism. Importantly, all three developed radical conceptions of art practice as collaborative & trans-medial, ranging from Gaudier's formal extrapolations of salvaged materials, to Paolozzi's mechano-morphisms, to Metzger's auto-destructive acid-&-nylon demonstrations, etcetera – each in tandem with the publication of manifestos &/or lecture performances. In Metzger's case, art practice merged directly into social practice through his involvement with the Committee for Nuclear Disarmament, the Direct Action Committee Against Nuclear War & the Committee of 100 – thereby generalising Kurt Schwitter's advocacy of the "unity of art & non-art."[25] Metzger's mid-1960s collaboration with poet Bob Cobbing, for the DIAS (Destruction in Art) Symposium at Better Books on Charring Cross Road – like the exchanges between Gaudier & Ezra Pound that fuelled *Blast* – along with the Independent Group's ICA lectures & the work around the 1956 "This is Tomorrow" exhibition at the Whitechapel Gallery, are likewise not only indicative of a socially-grounded practice, but one that repudiates the facile equivalence of aesthetic autonomy with individualism.

---

[24] See e.g. Jeff Nuttall, *Bomb Culture* (London: Paladin, 1970).
[25] Qtd in Andrew Wilson, "Gustav Metzger's Auto-Destructive / Auto-Creative Art: An Art of Manifesto, 1959-1969," *Third Text* 22.2 (March 2008): 181.

That such practice is grounded in the re-use of ephemera & the production of categorically ambivalent artefacts, or non-artefacts (performances, interventions, auto-destructions), amplifies an intransigence towards *art work* as *productive of commodification*. This intransigence towards "surplus production," in which art (inadvertently or otherwise) announces its own obsolescence, was spelled out in a series of manifestos, culminating in Metzger's several statements on auto-destructive art. In the first of these, published in November 1959, Metzger writes: "Auto-destructive art is primarily a form of public art for industrial societies… When the disintegrative process is complete, the work is to be removed from the site & scrapped."[26] As economy-without-reserve, Metzger's auto-destructive *art work* echoes Gaudier's concept of the *vortex* as "INTENSITY OF LIFE BURSTING THE PLANE": a negation, by way of the "transformation of technology into public art," of the fetish economy of cultural "ruins."[27]

The Vortex of Production

Reflecting on Gaudier's "great achievement" during his four frenzied years in London, Ezra Pound noted: "It was done against the whole social system in the sense that it was done against poverty & the lack of materials."[28] The vehemence of establishment denunciations of Gaudier's experiments at the time (as with Bomberg's & Paolozzi's) wasn't an "aesthetic" stance, but one of cultural power intent on breaking what it couldn't seduce or expropriate.[29] Yet this struggle was also an impetus – as Gaudier wrote in a letter from 1910: "the more I wander about amidst filth & sweat the better I understand art & love it: the desire for it becomes my crying need." Like Paolozzi's collage assemblages of consumer admass or "Bunk" (satirico-critical counterparts to a sculptural practice involving welded scrap metal) – yet unlike, for example, the Constructions Murondins of Le Corbusier[30] – Gaudier's reliance on

---

[26] Qtd in Wilson, "Gustav Metzger's Auto-Destructive / Auto-Creative Art," 182.

[27] Gustav Metzger, "Second Manifesto of Auto-Destructive Art" (1060), qtd in Wilson, "Gustav Metzger's Auto-Destructive / Auto-Creative Art," 184.

[28] Qtd in Hugh Kenner, *The Pound Era* (Berkeley: University of California Press, 1971), 250. See also Ezra Pound, *A Memoir of Gaudier-Brzeska* (New York: New Directions, 1970).

[29] The war was its ideal instrument of enforced "disillusionment" in this respect.

[30] Le Corbusier – during the German occupation of France – conceived a series of projects using brick, rubble & wood, to which he referred by the neologism "murondins" (from *murs*, walls + *rondins*, logs). These constructions were characterized by an economy of means in part

"oddments of stone left over from other people's hackings"[31] presents a rebuke to what Ken Russell, in his 1972 film *Savage Messiah*, parodies as "art democracy": the secular worship of commodity fetishes (& its political debt culture – the *price* of this socalled democratic spirit in "art" as in "life"). In doing so, it orientates what Hito Steyerl (in a reversioning of Arte Povera & Jerzy Grotowsky's "poor theatre") calls the "poor image" – the work of materially degraded art – as *anti-work*.

Steyerl's "poor image" – echoing Gaudier's "sympathy" for the "barbaric peoples of the earth"[32] (in turn echoing the opening line of "L'Internationale" [1864]) – developed out of an extended reflection on Chris Marker & Third Cinema, & is described as "a copy in motion" – not simply the "motion" of digital images, or their circulation through the economy of technical reproduction, but the *motion* of a certain historicity. "The poor image," Steyerl writes, "is a rag or a rip… *a lumpen proletarian in the class society of appearances.*"[33] It is defined by "low" resolutions, where "low" needn't correspond to dpi. Most importantly, the poor image "is no longer about the real thing – the originary original. Instead, it is about its own real conditions of existence." As Grotowsky wrote in 1965, on the relationship of competing modes of spectacularism:

> Theatre must admit its limits. If it cannot be richer than film, then let it be poorer. If it cannot be as lavish as television, then let it be ascetic. If it cannot create an attraction on a technical level, then let it give up all artificial technique. All that is left is a "holy" actor in a poor theatre.[34]

Despite appearances, this isn't a mere strategy of "reaction." What matters in defining the "poor image" isn't a degradation of *content*, but a materiality of degradation itself, out of which arises the possibility of radical co-option. "By losing its visual substance," Steyerl proposes, the "poor image" creates around it a new *aura* – "no longer based on the permanence of the 'original,' but on the transience of the copy."[35] And

dictated by the near-at-hand & in part by the scarcity of building materials during the war, but for all other intents & purposes their orientation is that of a *recuperative productivism*.

[31] Kenner, *The Pound Era*, 250.
[32] Henri Gaudier-Brezska, "Mr Henri- Gaudier-Brezska on the New sculpture," *Egoist* 1.6 (March 1914): 117-18.
[33] Hito Steyerl, "In Defense of the Poor Image," *The Wretched of the Screen* (Berlin: Sternberg, 2012) 32.
[34] Jerzy Grotowsky, "The Theatre's New Testament," *Towards a Poor Theatre* (Stockholm: Grotowsky & Odin Theatrets Forlag, 1968) 32-33.
[35] Steyerl, "In Defense of the Poor Image," 42 – emphasis added.

we can go further, by insisting that this "copy" isn't a mimēsis in any straightforward sense, but the material "itself" in its ongoing co-option – whether Gaudier's pilfered gravestones, Paolozzi's *Bunk!* magazine cutouts, Metzger's *Cardboards*, or Steyerl's AVIs & jpegs.

This transient aura is, of course, the counterpart of the *aura of the commodity* – & it is this that confers upon the "poor image" a critical & not merely artefactual status. It is the aura that shimmers on the event horizon of lightspeed obsolescence: the implosion of *value itself* into garbage. The "poor image" evokes negentropy. In it, the alchemical illusionism of the commodity is "deformed" – via a cybernetics of impoverished labour – into the *stuff* of an active political constructivism. With it, too, a certain conception of "art" as *cultural antimatter*. But this seemingly recuperative movement can't simply be a matter of feeding commodification's shit back to it in the *magical* form of an aesthetic gold standard called "the institutional avantgarde," whose artefacts – like Pierro Manzoni's *Merda d'Artista* (1961) – ironically advert to the "puerile utopia"[36] of the deregulated cultural marketplace. Rather, it is a question, to paraphrase Courbet, of radical "democracy in art."[37] That is to say, of a certain "equivalence" of exchange, in which everything is equally abstracted before the law of value-production *as irrecuperable entropy*.

There is a belligerent egalitarianism that we encounter in Russell's *Savage Messiah*, viscerally at odds with the museumised cultural paternalism & art-for-the-masses which serves as the target of the film's relentless parody. In a highly polemical scene centred around an Easter Island monolith, Russell depicts the crushing institutional ambivalence of the Royal Academy (masquerading as the Louvre) in the form of a monumental ethnological exhibit of "primitive art." The scene concludes with Gaudier's physical ejection by museum guards after volubly eulogising the Easter Island head as living art embalmed in a colonial mortuary. It is paralleled later in the film by two other scenes: the first showing Gaudier exultantly jackhammering a version of "Red Stone Dancer" (1913) into some roadworks, to the cheers of construction workers, evocative of Epstein's "Rock Drill" of the same year & redolent of Metzger's Southbank acid-dissolve performances of the mid-60s; while the second shows Gaudier hurling his own "primitive" sculpture

---

[36] Charles Baudelaire, "Pierre Dupont," *Oeuvres Complètes*, ed. Y.-G. Le Dantec & C. Pichois (Paris: Gallimard, 1961) 614 – referring here specifically to the cult of art-for-art's-sake.

[37] Qtd in Linda Nochlin, *The Politics of Vision: Essays on Nineteenth-Century Art & Society* (New York: Harper & Row, 1989) 3.

through the front window of a London art dealer's gallery – the return, so to speak, of the "poor image" in the form of what Gaudier called the "PALEOLITHIC VORTEX."[38]

Russell's window-smashing scene is reminiscent of the filmmaker's other major treatment of cultural iconoclasm fed-back through the spectacle of disillusionment – *Tommy* (1975) – in which The Who's Roger Daltrey "breaks the mirror" of blinding false enlightenment, only to find himself martyrised by "the masses," who have been indelibly conditioned by the commodity's promise of instant gratification. But if Gaudier's work likewise "broke the mirror" of a prevailing conception of sculptural art ("an agglomeration of Rodin-Maillol & useless academism"),[39] the individual pieces themselves have – beyond the tributes of Pound, Ford Maddox Ford & a few others – tended to be discussed precisely for their *minority*, as mere indicators of a future possibility foreclosed by Gaudier's "premature" death at Neuville St Vaast in 1915 at the age of twenty three – "part," as Pound judiciously put it, "of the *war waste*"[40]:

> There died a myriad,
> And of the best, among them,
> For an old bitch gone in the teeth,
> For a botched civilization.[41]

This thematic carries over into a formal critique of the work itself. Indeed, the mark of Gaudier's "greatest innovation," so Marjorie Perloff tells us, is the "presentation of movement that is potential rather than actual."[42] A movement that seems to anticipate, in its directness of attack, a kineticism as yet unachieved – one unbounded by sculptural conventions not only of form but of material, & of a certain *material inertia* that will come to preoccupy that line of exploration from Calder & Maholy-Nagy to Richard Serra & Bruce Nauman. Yet already in Gaudier, it is a movement vested in the materiality of the "whole work" as a complex of situations – in which we must include the means & circumstances of its construction as well as its subsequent trajectory in the thought of 20th-century art: from Gaudier's forging of his own tools & eschewal of modelling, to the

[38] Henri Gaudier-Brzeska, "GAUDIER-BRZESKA VORTEX," *Blast* (June 1914), rpr. Pound, *Gaudier-Brzeska*, 20.
[39] Henri Gaudier-Brzeska, "Allied Artists Association Ltd." (1914), rpr. Pound, *Gaudier-Brzeska*, 32.
[40] Pound, *Gaudier-Brzeska*, 17 – emphasis added.
[41] Ezra Pound, "Hugh Selwyn Mauberley," *Selected Poems 1908-1959* (London: Faber, 1975) 101.
[42] Marjorie Perloff, *The Dance of the Intellect: Studies in the Poetry of the Pound Tradition* (Evanston: Northwestern University Press, 1996) 52.

cannibalism of quasi-industrial waste into aesthetico-critical "vortices." As Gaudier wrote in a 1912 letter to his partner Sophie Brzeska: "Movement is the translation of life, & if art depicts life, movement should come into art, since we are only aware of life because it moves."[43]

De-Fetishising Art-Work

Gaudier's dynamism steps away from that of the Futurists precisely in its refusal to relinquish the contemporary lifeworld for a mimetic techno-utopianism, while equally repudiating the retreat into Humanism that was to characterise Bomberg's sometimes reactionary stance following his experiences during WWI. In Gaudier, technicity is never separate from life (even as encountered in the trenches at Neuville St. Vaast), nor is it *exemplified* in the monumentality of industrialised, militarised social organisation or the march of progress & mass mechanised warfare. If Gaudier's work is to be regarded as "minor" &/or "potential" – or, so to speak, *poor* – this in itself isn't incidental but rather the substance of a praxis whose *movement* describes a series of vectors:

1. from economic circumstances to an economy of circumstance;
2. from economy of circumstance to critical method (virtue of necessity);
3. from critical method to the materiality of critique (a gravestone, cut brass, a rifle butt);
4. culminating in the deconstruction of the art/life dichotomy as *work* (the Vortex).

In many respects, Gaudier's anti-aestheticism anticipates Dada's open assault on the fetishising of what Clement Greenberg will later call *medium*. For Gaudier, as with Schwitters (whose *Merz* constructions are nothing if not a restatement of the paleolithic vortex), there is only *material*. It is for this reason, too, that Gaudier's "sculpture" can't be reduced to the mimetic/phenomenal dichotomy presented in Gotthold Lessing's *Lacoön*, with which Rosalind Krauss begins her reconsideration of avantgarde sculpture from Boccioni to Nauman (a book which notably omits any mention of Gaudier, Epstein, Schwitters, Paolozzi or Metzger). "Sculpture is an art," Lessing writes, "concerned with the deployment of bodies in space… This defining spatial characteristic must be separated from the essence of those artforms, like poetry, whose medium is time."

---

[43] H.S. Ede, *Savage Messiah: A Biography of the Sculptor Henri Gaudier-Brzeska* (London: Kettle's Yard & Henry Moore Institute, 1931).

However, he adds, "all bodies exist not only in space but also in time. They continue, & at any moment of their continuance may assume a different appearance & stand in a different relation."[44] Yet in Gaudier, as in the work of Schwitters, Paolozzi & Metzger, such spatiotemporal coordinates are never *separate* from a broadly social movement (i.e. in collective tension) – in particular the circulation of commodities in which a certain *ambivalence* predominates, in the exchange of "value" & "non-value," where "History," "abstraction" & "alienation" intersect.

Here, in its ongoing critique of aesthetic morality ("the good & the beautiful"), Courbet's "proletarian" radical democracy collides with the ultimate dross: the commodity itself. If for Steyerl "poor images are the contemporary Wretched of the Screen,"[45] for Courbet the "poor image" is the image of the socially "unpresentable":

> Poor images are poor because they are not assigned any value within the class society of images – their status as illicit or degraded grants them exemption from its criteria.[46]

That the one can be made to collapse into the other should alert us to the significance of Gaudier's project, in which what is at stake is rather the *unpresentable as such*. This doesn't mean a *reification* of social relations into a working material (something that is the accomplishment of industrialisation, in fact), but of an articulation of that which escapes (or is suppressed by) the ideology of mimēsis. Insofar as the relationship between the "poor image" & the "unpresentable" mirrors a return of the commodity's magical evanescence to the base materiality of some *thing* (i.e. garbage), it serves to demystify those political seductions of "emancipation" proffered by regimes of socalled "representation." Such were the prevailing conditions under which Saint-Simon evoked the idea of a revolutionary avantgarde to "spread new ideas" & exercise a "positive power over society,"[47] in contest with those property codes dictating which "ideas" in art were to be communicated. Moreover, with Napoléon III's inauguration of the Salon des Réfuses in 1863, this nascent avantgarde had to contend with its own (instantaneous) institutionalisation – that

---

[44] Qtd in Rosalind Krauss, *Passages in Modern Sculpture* (Cambridge, MA: MIT Press, 1977) 3-4.
[45] Steyerl, "In Defense of the Poor Image," 32.
[46] Steyerl, "In Defense of the Poor Image," 38.
[47] Henri de Saint-Simon, *Opinions littéraires, philosophiques et industrielles* (Paris, 1825), ctd in Donald D. Egbert, "The Idea of the 'Avantgarde' in Art & Politics," *The American Historical Review* 73.2 (December 1967): 343.

infinitesimal temporality in which the *work* of the avantgarde returns to being alienated cultural labour.[48]

The vertiginous transmutation of social dross into class consciousness into social democracy thus becomes the commodified appeal of upward mobility by way of *free* commerce. Likewise the inauguration of a space of aesthetic "refusal" provided a surrogate for political radicalism, seeking to diffuse the force of the avantgarde in an all-encompassing (homeostatic) pluralism while proffering the illusion of its autonomy only to the extent of its expropriation & commodification. What emerges from the subsequent *disillusionment* of the avantgarde – from Dada to the Nouveaux Réalistes (who Metzger first polemicised against as surrendering "the world in its totality as work of art" for the sake of commercialisation[49]) – is a socially-critical art that increasingly mines the commodity's underside, its dirty secret, its "unpresented": that armature of dross on which the aura of its allure is sustained. It's in this respect that the intensities of Gaudier's otherwise "attenuated" project amount to something like a Minimanual of Urban Guerrilla Art, whose legacy persists – via the détournements & dérives of the Lettrists, Situationists & Fluxus – in such "samizdat counter-histories" as Laura Oldfield Ford's *Savage Messiah* London zine series from 2005-2009.

Entropy is the Mirror of Abstraction

Borrowing (like Russell) the title of Jim Ede's 1931 biography of Gaudier, Ford's *Savage Messiah* is a self-consciously lo-fi assemblage of "collaged & photocopied pages" – redolent of Paolozzi's April 1952 *Bunk* epidiascope performance at the ICA (assembled from American magazine cut-outs, postcards, diagrams, & assorted admass) – recording the artist's drift through neoliberalism's border zones in post-Blairite London: "lanes of traffic, toxic troughs… glyphs in a spiral stairway, a submerged arcade… a loophole, a hidden anomaly."[50] As with Paolozzi, "objects from the environment become the collage-skins of the beings in that environment."[51]

---

[48] Of which there are strange echoes in the dispute between Marx & Bakunin between 1868 & 1872, in the context of which Bakunin convened a Social Democratic Alliance as a revolutionary avantgarde *within the First International*, resulting in a split that divided the revolutionary movement for many years.

[49] Wilson, "Gustav Metzger's Auto-Destructive / Auto-Creative Art," 189.

[50] Laura Oldfield Ford, "Scorched Earth," *ArtReview* (October 2015): artreview.com/opinion/October_2015_opinion_laura_oldfield_ford/

[51] Qtd in John-Paul Stonard, "Used Future: The Early Sculptures of Eduardo Paolozzi," *Eduardo Paolozzi. Archaeology of a Used Future: Sculpture 1946-1959* (London: John Clark Fine Art, 1959) 26.

Ford's subject is both "a city in the process of being buried" beneath the accumulated mass of industrialised image-manipulation & a poetics of salvage of London's "negative equity ghettos" (a re-weirding of gentrification processes productive of *futured ruins*, evoking the metamorphic urban sculpture of China Miéville's *Un Lun Dun*).

Savage Messiah, in Ford's words, is a "mapping of ruptures like the London riots, the breaks in the flattened time of a 'continuous present.'"[52] Like Gaudier's found, appropriated & stolen bits of cultural "hackings" & Metzger's "auto-destructive" erasures, Ford's materials are the "punks, squatters, ravers, football hooligans & militants," as Mark Fisher writes in a preface to the later book edition, "left behind by a history which has ruthlessly photoshopped them out of its finance-friendly SimCity."[53] For Fisher, *Savage Messiah* is permeated by a Derridean "hauntology": "the idea of being haunted by lost futures." In this sense it self-consciously situates itself within that *anachronistic* fissure defining the avantgarde, between the recuperation of a radical impulse & the future-imaginary reduced to expired commodities. In doing so it recalls the ambivalence of the "poor image," whose circulation, Steyerl reminds us, "feeds into both capitalist media assembly lines & alternative audiovisual communities":

> The poor image – ambivalent as its status may be – thus takes its place in the genealogy of carbon-copied pamphlets, cine-train agitprop films, underground video magazines & other nonconformist materials…[54]

Moreover, as Steyerl goes on to argue, the poor image "*reactualises* many of the historical ideas associated with these circuits…"[55] They serve, in a manner of speaking, as the constellational logic of the "vernacular spolia of reality"[56] they embody. In doing so, they conjoin the ideas of Gaudier (vortex), Eisenstein (montage) & Benjamin (dialectical image), but also William Burroughs who, as Fisher notes, "deploys collage" in much the

---

[52] Interview with Rosanna McLaughlin, "Laura Oldfield Ford: 'I map ruptures…,'" *Studio International* (9 February 2017): www.studiointernational.com/index.php/laura-oldfield-ford-interview-i-map-ruptures-london-riots

[53] Mark Fisher, "Always Yearning for the Time That Just Eluded Us," introduction to Laura Oldfield Ford, *Savage Messiah* (London: Verso, 2011).

[54] Steyerl, "In Defense of the Poor Image," 43-44.

[55] Steyerl, "In Defense of the Poor Image," 44 – emphasis mine.

[56] Michael Leiris, "Contemporary Sculptors VII – Thoughts Around Giacometti," trans. Douglas Cooper, *Horizon* 19 (June 1949): 411-17.

same way as Ford, "as a weapon in time-war."⁵⁷ In the June 1914 issue of *Blast*, Gaudier wrote:

> Sculptural energy is the mountain.
> Sculptural feeling is the appreciation of masses in relation.
> Sculptural ability is the defining of these masses by planes…
> PLASTIC SOUL IS INTENSITY OF LIFE BURSTING THE PLANE.⁵⁸

For Gaudier, the deconstruction of the "Law of Genre"⁵⁹ defined by socalled historical necessity is indeed a form of time-war against the abolition of a future that is forever presenting itself in the institutionalisation & normalisation of art *as the permanent tension between praxis & reification*.⁶⁰ And if "the whole history of sculpture" thus feeds, as Perloff asserts, into a "complete revaluation of form as a means of expression,"⁶¹ this isn't for the purpose of aesthetic novelty, but as an affirmation of the *possible* through a deconstruction of the *permitted*. Gaudier's "working-class avantgardism" isn't a *primitivism*: his "PALEOLITHIC VORTEX" is the antithesis of regression; moreso the antithesis of a seeking after exotic forms of authenticity. It is rather a "bursting" of the plane of a supervening present – the collapsed present-time of the commodity – into the future-anterior of the "new, primordial."⁶² In other words, a work of *dis-alienation*.

Like Paolozzi & Ford's differing examinations of rampant commodification – as the major socially-transformative force of the post-War era – Gaudier's & Metzger's methods transform the working environment (London) from a series of private & institutional demarcations of *property* into an eruptive vortex of possibilities resistant to the very idea of ownership. And if "sculpture & architecture are one & the same,"⁶³ as Gaudier argued, then the critique of art equally extends to those systems of regulation & control that fuse urbanism with the cultural heritage industry, as quiescent real-estate décor – a critical line

---

⁵⁷ Fisher, "Always Yearning for the Time That Just Eluded Us."
⁵⁸ "GAUDIER-BRZESKA VORTEX," rpr. Pound, *Gaudier-Brzeska*, 21.
⁵⁹ See Jacques Derrida, "The Law of Genre," trans. Avital Ronell, in *Acts of Literature*, ed. Derek Attridge (London: Routledge, 1992) 223ff.
⁶⁰ The introjection of this movement, by which the temporality of commodification is brought into view, subsequently marks that point at which avantgarde art-work displaces the a-temporal logic of the "artwork."
⁶¹ Perloff, *The Dance of the Intellect*, 54.
⁶² Gaudier-Brzeska, "Allied Artists Association Ltd.," 31.
⁶³ Gaudier-Brzeska, "Allied Artists Association Ltd.," 30.

that likewise extends through the psychogeographies of Ralph Rumney, Stewart Home, Marc Atkins & Iain Sinclair; the site-specific political performance art of Stuart Brisley; as well as Wolf Vostell's "Dé-coll/age Architecture" (1961) & other works included in Vostell & Dick Higgins' 1969 volume *Fantastic Architecture*; & in the deconstructive practice of the Anarchitecture Group (Gordon Matta-Clark, Laurie Anderson, Tina Girouard, et al.; 1973).

The sculptural-architectural vortex is nothing if not the transverse movement of psychogeographic *détournement* itself, its radical collage-effect wrought upon the organisational structures of the aesthetic/social complex & their instrumentalist logic. This is the predominant function assigned by Guy Debord to the Situationist *dérive*, as a praxis of urbanological deconstruction. The *dérive*, as defined by Debord, is "a technique of transient passage through varied ambiances" entailing "playful-constructive behaviour" distinguishing it from notions associated with the Baudelairean flâneur. It seeks to subvert "the domination of psychogeographical variations" & to exploit a "calculation of their possibilities"[64] in counterpoint to the forces of urban planning – just as Gaudier & others worked in a constructive counterpoint to the forces of aesthetic normalisation vis-à-vis the "objectivity" of sculpture.

"I think about walking in the city," says Ford, "as a way of unlocking memory, of encountering time slips, dreams & desires." The temporal physiognomy of Ford's urban *détournements* mirrors the collage-effect of Gaudier's spatial reconfigurations of material & environment in the evolution of works such as "Bird Swallowing a Fish," "Fish," & "Torpedo Fish (Toy)" (all produced in 1914). Like Ford's *Savage Messiah*, Gaudier's project can similarly be read as nothing if not *anti-utopian*. His "walks, his prowls, his constant chipping at stone,"[65] as Pound recounts, synthesise a relation of abstract elements to a whole social praxis – recalling Ivan Chteglov's "Formulary for a New Urbanism" (1953): "Dreams spring from reality & are realised in it."[66]

> All cities are geological; you cannot take three steps without encountering ghosts bearing all the prestige of their legends. We move within a *closed* landscape whose landmarks constantly draw us toward the past. Certain

---

[64] Guy Debord, "Theory of the Dérive," *Situationist International Anthology*, ed. & trans. Ken Knabb (Berkeley: Bureau of Public Secrets, 1981) 50.

[65] Pound, *Gaudier-Brzeska*, 40.

[66] Ivan Chteglov, "Formulary for a New Urbanism" (1953), *Situationist International Anthology*, 2.

shifting angles, certain *receding* perspectives, allow us to glimpse original conceptions of space, but this vision remains fragmentary. [...] It has become essential to bring about a complete spiritual transformation by bringing to light forgotten desires & by creating entirely new ones. And by carrying out an *intensive propaganda* in favour of these desires.[67]

Chteglov's unitary urbanism revives the delirium of the Paris Commune, suggesting that the revolutionary artist should take up their tools the way one takes up arms against the institutional forces of entropy. Similarly, Gaudier's & Ford's architectonics of sub-cultural *refuse* transforms the work of salvage – like Metzger's auto-destructive/auto-creative "manifestations" or Paolozzi's "Bunk" & found-film works (e.g. *History of Nothing*, 1962) – into a refusal of the *un*presentable against the totality of what, within a system of mimetic domination that Kenneth Clark (in a syntax ridiculed by Russell) could still, in the wake of two world wars, grandiosely call Civilisation.

Avantgardism & the Cybernetic Predicament

It is this project of wilful "barbarism," of a "revolt against civilisation," that radicalises the concept of *art-work* in the line of attack developed from Gaudier to Paolozzi, Metzger, Ford, & which points also to a renewal of Courbet's notion of an avantgarde beyond the spiral of formal innovation & aesthetic novelty into which – in the recursive "détournements" of postmodernism – it had threatened to descend, & to which Bürger subsequently sees it as inevitably succumbing, post-WW2, in the institutionalism of what he terms the "neo-avantgarde." Indeed, the direction in which Gaudier's work points is that of an "end of culture" itself – whether understood as class, genre, stereotype or division of labour – & a remaking of "art" from its ruins. To this extent, commodification isn't a negation but a primordial force (of signifying social separation) that *makes possible* this movement. It is never a question – in the subsequent tendencies of Paolozzi & Metzger – of retreating from abstraction, as Bomberg had done (in a rejection of Marinetti's bombastic techno-futurist militarism), but of grasping its broadest ramifications *as a categorical equivalence of exchange between all constituent elements*[68] – aesthetic, social, political, technological, ontological. It was only on the level of abstraction, in fact, that the

[67] Chteglov, "Formulary for a New Urbanism," 1-3.
[68] Of which Humanism, also, is one.

avantgarde could critique (or in Situationist terms, *détourne*) the commodity form & the ideological system that has sought to maintain a monopoly over it *as the constitutive form of everyday life*. Precisely because it is only on the level of abstraction that the categorical reason vested in the commodity is contradicted by it.

It is for this reason that Bürger misconstrues the relation of (anti-)*work* to the concept of *functionlessness*. The avantgarde, he argues, counters functionlessness "not by an art that would have consequences within the existing society, but rather by the principles of sublation of art in the praxis of life."[69] In other words, by drawing from the equivalence of the *impoverishment of aesthetic labour* an impetus that directly aligns with that of a broadly social-revolutionary tendency, in which the concept of the social nevertheless remains in a fixed constellation. In Bürger's terms, this means displacing *alienation*, as the "content" of art-work, with the *sublation* of art-work itself (defined in solely "negative" terms, i.e. functionlessness). The avantgarde thus corresponds to a specific transformation of theory into praxis, of which neoavantgarde art would be the transient "false consciousness."

Yet it is meaningless under such conditions to continue to insist (as Bürger does) upon the rhetorical distinction between "art & the praxis of life."[70] Just as it is meaningless to speak of "autonomous" artwork as the production of/by "individualities," since the production of autonomy (abstraction) is itself the product of a general logic that is both an "aesthetic" & a "technē politikē" (since Bürger's "individuality" is simply a mystification, as we've already seen, of an alienation that is itself *constitutive* of subjectivity). It is the *system of abstraction* that produces the *work of autonomy*, & does so – as cybernetics makes abundantly plain – in an *ambivalent* relation to the Humanism that continues to haunt every art/life dichotomy (as the self-sufficiency of alienated thought & the arbitrary commerce of its significations).[71] The seemingly historical character of these antagonisms already belies the technical character of historicism itself, as what Eisenstein called the "montage of attractions"[72] & what Derrida has called "the *polysemy* of technē."[73]

---

[69] Bürger, *Theory of the Avant-Garde*, 51.

[70] Bürger, *Theory of the Avant-Garde*, 51.

[71] "Alienated thought is always sufficient unto itself." Raoul Vaneigem, *The Movement of the Free Spirit*, trans. Randall Cherry & Ian Patterson (New York: Zone Books, 1994) 13.

[72] See Sergei Eisenstein, "The Montage of Attractions," *Eisenstein Reader* (London: British Film Institute, 1998) 35ff.

[73] Jacques Derrida, *The Truth in Painting*, trans. Geoff Bennington & Ian McLeod (Chicago: Chicago University Press, 1987) 21 – emphasis added.

Though computers are almost universally synonymous with logic & functionality, & have increasingly become the very paradigm of reason itself, displacing that of "Man," this has been accomplished under the paradoxical sign of a technological mysticism that only appears to be the inverse of a Humanist "aesthetic." Which is to say, as the aestheticisation of reason. In the figure of the computer, the entire history of technical artefacts is aggregated into a unified system of rationalised control & communication: in the period around WW2, what throughout previous history had been regarded simply as *prostheses* were abruptly transformed through systematisation into something like an *autonomous agency* in which the two apparently opposed Messianisms of civilisation & progress intersect. Thus while in appearance a centuries-old Humanist standpoint was displaced with remarkably little resistance by a technocentric one, in truth they are indistinguishable. It is no surprise, then, that in the half-century since the foundation of cybernetics as a discipline, electronic digital computers & a rapidly evolving AI have not only "infiltrated" to the most trivial levels of everyday reality, they effectively constitute the very *means of production* of reality itself.

How did this happen?[74]

---

[74] It had long been suspected, contrary to certain organicist & theological notions, that "life" as previously understood wasn't a category apart from "technology" – & that what had been called "mind" devolved not upon vague metaphysical concepts but upon a definable mechanics of self-organisation & self-modification in physical systems. Such an autopoiēsis provided the framework for a "general intelligence," whose lineaments might be detected in one form or another universally – whether in the behaviour of other species of "animal," or in the biosphere at large, or in the characteristics of subatomic particles – but above all in a continuum with socalled *artificial* intelligence. As we all know, this was elegantly demonstrated in Alan Turing's restaging of a certain mimetic allegory – the elder Pliny's famous "grapes & drapes" test of Zeuxis & Parrhasius. What Pliny presented as a contest between art (technē) & nature is reduced in Turing's *Imitation Game* to the act of judgement itself: in this case between "man & machine" (or, considering its – & Turing's – gendered history, *trans* & machine). What this act of judgement reveals, however, is a fundamental *ambivalence*, vested as it is in the entirely implicated figure of the *artist*, the *scientist*, & the *interrogator*. A judgement, in other words, situated at the intersection of an aesthetic, scientific & political *knowledge* more than able to "deceive" itself – not through some technical insufficiency, but because the very distinction it is supposed to test is a product of its own logical operations. In its capacity to see itself reflected in all things, judgement *as such* (its fundamental lability) becomes the predicate of a generalised *cybernetics*. As in Pliny's allegory, the question is no longer one of content (the *what* in which "nature," or the "artist," is deceived), but of a co-dependency of *contradiction, paradox, indeterminacy*. We might speak, rather, of a kind of *mimetic algorithm*: not a mimēsis of any *thing*, or *concept* (the imitation of "the human" by "the machine," for example), but of *mimēsis itself*, in the conditional (or rather probabilistic) form of an *as if*. And this would necessarily include proceeding *as if* the world were susceptible to a *rationality*

Such facets of cybernetics contribute significantly to the view that, rather than representing a break with the aesthetics & positivist science of modernity, it constitutes an extension of it, through the *putting to work* of the previously *unpresentable* & *irrational* in the form of a generalised, technical *system*. In this, cybernetics bears certain resemblances to the "positivism" of psychoanalysis, semiotics & the cubo-futurist-constructivist avantgarde. It is no accident that cognition, communication & creativity preoccupied cybernetics from the outset, in the attempt to simulate a human hypothesis, but more-so as analogues to the fundamentally cybernetic problem of "general intelligence" (an expression which translates equally well to "everyday life"). Such preoccupations served not only to strategically "humanise" cybernetics – which in any case had a long pre-history of anthropomorphic curiosities, like Kempelen's chess-playing "Turk" – but, in its more sinister aspirations, to engineer various beguiling systems of what José Delgado termed "psychocivilization": the extension of power-through-information, to power-through-behavioural-control, to the eventual *production* of collective & individual consciousness.[75] A species of automatised Panopticism built into the fabric of "everyday life."

In 1969 Delgado published *Physical Control of the Mind: Toward a Psychocivilized Society*, which extrapolated from isolated research on remote electro-stimulation of the brain to an entire authoritarian social machinery. Where Delgado envisaged the need for physical mutilation, the emerging industry in Public Relations envisaged semantic reprogramming through the pervasive feedback system of mass media & the stimulation of *irrational consumer impulses* which themselves could be commodified. Between the advancement of a technochratic security state & commodity capitalism – what Wheeler contemporaneously referred to as the "universal revolution" of cybernetics[76] – the social application of such apparently dehumanising technologies required an alibi. It sought

---

premised upon acts of judgement, decision, critique & *ipso facto* that this underlying rationality of the world qualifies such acts of judgement, decision, critique as inherently *rational*. Such is the tautological "nature" of the cybernetic hypothesis issuing from Turing's "game," as a kind of simulacral or *trans-* Newtonianism. In this way such excluded features of Newtonian mechanics as chaos & complexity are able not only to be *modelled* but to be statistically & topologically *determined* in such a way as to permit their representation both within & by series of cybernetic operations.

[75] José Delgado, *Physical Control of the Mind: Toward a Psychocivilized Society* (New York: Harper & Row, 1969).

[76] Wheeler, *Democracy in a Revolutionary Era*, 14.

this, as it continues to seek it, in the domain of "culture," & such may be said to be the substance of the 1968 "Cybernetic Serendipity" exhibition at London's ICA.[77]

As a landmark moment in the integration of the contemporary arts & sciences, "Cybernetic Serendipity" displayed an attitude towards innovation which combined that of major industrial fairs (it attracted some 40,000 visitors before transferring to the Corcoran Gallery in Washington & the San Francisco Exploratorium) with the subversive avantgardism of such precursors as the "Man, Machine & Motion" group exhibition at the Hatton Gallery in 1955 & "This is Tomorrow" at the Whitechapel Gallery a year later (both vehicles of the Independent Group around Paolozzi & Hamilton). As curator Jasia Reichardt explained, the exhibition intended to showcase "artists' involvement with science, &… scientists' involvement with the arts" as well as "the links between the random systems employed by artists, composers & poets, & those involved with the making & the use of cybernetic devices." Moreover, it sought to do so in a "positive social & political climate," under the auspices of Harold Wilson's aggressively "white heat of technology" Labour government,[78] playing to the "dream of technical control & of instant information conveyed at unthought-of velocities" which pervaded 1960s culture.[79]

"Cybernetic Serendipity," in other words, sought not only to be timely, but to be both populist & experimental, to operate – in a manner of speaking – at the intersection of art, cybernetics & life. To accomplish

---

[77] Running from 1 August until 20 October, "Cybernetic Serendipity" opened just over a month after student & worker insurrections in Paris had brought French industry & government to the verge of collapse, averted at the last instant by snap parliamentary elections. Similar "disturbances" occurred in Mexico, Tokyo, the United States &, under seemingly inverted political circumstances, in Czechoslovakia (where the very first "Computer Art" exhibition occurred earlier that same year, in Brno, curated by the 21-year-old Jiří Valoch). The common element was an authoritarianism as *anachronistic* as the popular "revolutionary" impulses appealed to in resisting it. In Paris, acolytes of Situationism called not for a revolution in "everyday life": creative emancipation in place of the alienation of industrial labour. Yet if *this* revolution was said to have failed, it did so only as the advance guard of a more subtle "universal revolution": the cybernetic displacement of conventional authoritarianism by an ever more pervasive *soft power*, & the recuperation by a renewed Corporate-State Apparatus of the idea of creative emancipation via a new market in lifestyle choices.

[78] Catherine Mason, "Cybernetic Serendipity: History & Lasting Legacy," *Studio International* (11 March 2018): studiointernation.com/index.php/cybernetic-serendipity-history-&-lasting-legacy

[79] Edward A. Shanken, "From Cybernetics to Telematics: The Art, Pedagogy & Theory of Roy Ascott," in Roy Ascott, *Telematic Embrace: Visionary Theories of Art, Technology, & Consciousness* (Berkeley: University of California Press, 2003).

this within the institutional setting of the ICA required that the exhibition not only exemplify contemporary cybernetic cultural research, but also "subvert" the austere, menacing & even apocalyptic image of computers & atom-age technology handed down from 1950s science fiction – an image reprised in the figure of the psychopathic Heuristic Algorithmic mainframe in Stanley Kubrick's *2001: A Space Odyssey* of the same year. The inclusion of artists like Metzger, Bruce Lacey, Nam June Paik & Jean Tinguely – whose various works exhibited strong cyber-critical as well as cyber-positive impulses (through parody, satire & auto-destruction) – appears in this respect a calculated effort to co-opt avantgarde strategies to the service of dis-alienating the public from the abstract technologies of the Corporate-State Apparatus.

Stereotype as Operative Logic

In contrast to what has often been perceived as the dehuminising means-ends rationalism of social cyberneticisation, the construction of satirical-critical "machines" – from Paolozzi's mechano-morphic sculptures to Metzger & Tinguely's auto-productive/destructive installations, to the anthropo-robotics of Paik & Lacey – not only posed questions about what machines *are* & what they are *for*, but about the ideological character of machine aesthetics & machine culture generally – & about how machines may evolve beyond the limits of conventional predictive modelling in the future. Above all – & against the supposed "neutrality" of cybernetics as techno-scientific discourse – the satirical-critical character of auto-destructive art exposes its inherently *political* dimensions (perceived most visibly in the increased cyberneticisation of the "individual" & society at large throughout the post-WW2 period).

With the revolution in personal computers (& an accessible means of production of "computer art") still a decade away, "Cybernetic Serendipity" posed the "problem" of cybernetics not as a social & political one,[80] but as an aesthetic problem contained within the history of experimental art. The menacing intrusion of inexplicable new technologies into everyday life could thus be normalised as *spectacle*, restoring to the collective

---

[80] In any case, not a "scientific" problem: in public discourse the word "science" is ostensibly meaningless, other than in terms of immediate application in everyday experience. The public-at-large has neither the competence nor the inclination to concern themselves with socalled scientific problems, which must first be represented to them by other means, such as Industrial Fairs, science fiction, & the mass market in gadgets & labour-saving devices.

imagination the illusion of "power" over that which was designed to regulate & control human behaviour. Lacey's contribution to "Cybernetic Serendipity" is a case in point: a minimally anthropomorphic robot named R.O.S.A.B.O.S.O.M., designed to convey a Duchampian sense of futility & disarray in the technofetishisation of desire (Eros). Lacey's R.O.S.A. was designed to operate as a pair with another robot, M.A.T.E., which – using ultrasonic & infrared sensors – was programmed to automatically detect R.O.S.A.'s presence & follow her. Reuben Hoggett describes the ritual thus:

> As he gets closer to ROSA his infrared beam is activated, & ROSA has a corresponding detector. As he gets still closer, ROSA emits a scream from a tape-recorder stored within her body. MATE has a voice operated switch activated by the scream, & changes direction to avoid contact with her. If, however, the avoidance action doesn't quite work & they contact, Bruce installed contact switches on ROSA, & when activated (by MATE), she blows confetti everywhere. Bruce goes on to explain that after the courtship, the confetti is symbolic of ROSA & MATE being married.[81]

Counter-intuitively, an artificial intelligence is one that learns by breaking down, rather than simply through the positive aggregation of data. In their 1972 study of capitalism & schizophrenia, *Anti-Oedipus*, Gilles Deleuze & Félix Guattari identified the operation of "breakthroughs & breakdowns" with the fundamental drives of what, in an allusion to Duchamp's mechanical bride ("La mariée mise à nu par ses célibataires, même," 1915-1923),[82] they termed "desiring machines." For Lacey, such cybernetic allegories remain first & foremost allegories of a heteronormative "human" predicament: "Given a brain," Lacey writes, "man has the possibility of developing into a sublime, happy, creative, & unique creature, but he is prevented from realising his potential by the severe limitations imposed on him by the environment he has created for himself…"[83] To survive in the future, "he must rebuild his cities, rewrite his laws, & re-educate himself… He must do all of these things to suit his emotional, sexual & psychological needs."[84]

Lacey's desiring machines, like Tinguely's "Metamécaniques" & Metzger's auto-destructive/auto-creative sculptures, resembled automatised

---

[81] Reuben Hoggett, "1967 – MATE for R.O.S.A.B.O.S.O.M. – Bruce Lacey" (2009): www.cyberneticzoo.com.

[82] See Marshall McLuhan, *The Mechanical Bride: Folklore of Industrial Man* (London: Duckworth, 1951).

[83] Bruce Lacey, "On the Human Predicament," *Cybernetic Serendipity*, 38.

[84] Lacey, "On the Human Predicament," 39.

junk: a critical anti-aesthetic of emergent cyberculture. Tinguely's "cyclomatic" & "metamitic" painting machines & Metzger's "acid action paintings" were likewise designed not as an aestheticisation of randomness or of quasi-cybernetic processes, but as autopoiētic assemblages of generative perturbation – of *breakthroughs & breakdowns*. In contrast to the conventional aesthetics of "machine art" (like Roy E. Allen's "Patternmaker"), Tinguely's "metamitics" & Metzger's "acid paintings" produced *patterns* that were exactly neither "regular & repeatable"[85] nor objectively stable, but which produced, as Perloff says, a complete revaluation of form as a means of expression. In this they exploded the myth of a "primitivist" *art informel* (the socalled expressive fallacy) as a *negation* of abstract rationalism. In his 1964 article "On Random Activity in Material/Transforming Works of Art," Metzger stated that "at a certain point, the work takes over, is an activity beyond the detailed control of the artist, reaches a power, grace, momentum, transcendence… which the artist could not achieve except through random activity."[86] In doing so, these works likewise exposed the ideological fallacy behind "functionalist" cyber-aesthetics as well as the constructed "Humanism" of informal or expressive art, which now appeared interconnected[87] (as Willem de Kooning famously insisted, "style is a fraud"[88]).

Here, too, we see that Bürger's assertion about the avantgarde representing the "radical negation of the category of individual creation" is contradicted by the abstract ambivalence of Metzger's, Lacey's & Tinguely's work to the very category of individuality (the position of an "autonomous agency" that can potentially be occupied by *anything whatsoever*: the agency of a "class consciousness," for example, or of "revolutionary knowledge"). From this seemingly radical position (one which derived, in fact, from the convergence of Marx, Freud, Saussure & others), the avantgarde could be seen to challenge the dogmatic & essentialist tendencies disguised within the institutionalisation of art – as not merely ideological embellishments of power, but as indicative of a foundational logic. Yet it is precisely for this reason that it is wrong to speak, as Bürger does, of a "failure" of the avantgarde "to sublate art" into

---

[85] Roy E. Allen, "Mechanical Patternmaker," *Cybernetic Serendipity*, 40.
[86] Gustav Metzger, "On Random Activity in Material/Transforming Works of Art," *Signal News Bulletin of the Centre for Advanced Creative Study* 1.2 (30 July 1964).
[87] A pseudo-dichotomy which by 1968 was productive of nothing but cliché in any case.
[88] Willem de Kooning, "A Desperate View," talk delivered 18 February 1949 at Subjects of the Artist: A New Art School, 25 East 8th Street, New York City: www.dekooning.org/documentation/words/a-desperate-view

a life-praxis on the principle that its artefacts (its "manifestations") are subsequently recuperable for a general algorithmics of commodification. "The revival of art as an institution," Bürger insists, "& the revival of the category of 'work' suggest that, today, the avantgarde is already historical."[89] Such an observation is in any case rendered trivial by the fact that the commodity itself is the formal expression, *par excellence*, of abstract ambivalence, whose tactical availability to the critique (or production) of "value" (even as *non-value*) – as the cybernetic reconstitution of aesthetic labour exemplifies – remains open-ended.

The problem posed by the work of Metzger, Paolozzi, Gaudier *et al.*, is one in which the apparent antagonisms of techno-poiēsis are not discretely dissolved but rather generalised within the logic of work itself (as irrecuperable entropy). Like Nietzsche's laughter, this *excessive* movement – general, inflationary, satirical – threatens to destroy its sense (of productive subordination), to dislocate it from a recuperative logic *in general*, causing the very totalising movement that defines it to appear as what Bataille calls a "small comic recapitulation."[90] This concerns also the ability of cybernetic systems, as the mechano-morphic analogue of Gaudier's PALEOLITHIC VORTEX, not only to produce "active stereotypes" or nascent archetypes, but to represent what History teaches us to call the "unpresentable" – that indeterminate dynamic with which, in the last instance, humanity vests its innermost drives: as if, robbed of its unique claim upon reason, it had sought tactical advantage in the *irrational*. Far from exhausting the idea of an *autonomous* avantgarde, this movement exposes the dependency of all institutional structures upon an accelerated, convulsive movement of expropriation & recuperation that only bears the *semblance* of systematicity, but is in fact purely reactive to a paranoid, schizophrenic degree.

In this, Gaudier, Paolozzi & Metzger anticipate the totalising capacity of the cyberneticised Corporate-State Apparatus – signalled by the advent of the Organisation Man[91] – to produce an abstract reality in which individual & collective subjectivities are constituted as data aggregation which is fed back into the social economy in the ambivalent ritual guise of *either* "desiring" commodity-consumption *or* "revolutionary knowledge" – where the premium commodity is social being itself, in all its stereotyped idiosyncrasies. In this ideal synthesis of "art" (technē)

---

[89] Bürger, *Theory of the Avant-Garde*, 57.
[90] Georges Bataille, *L'expérience intérieure* (Paris: Gallimard, 1943) 60.
[91] See William H. Whyte, *The Organization Man* (New York: Simon & Schuster, 1956).

& "life," the aestheticisation of politics as Benjamin foresaw it is indistinguishable from a mystification of History as "technology" – where technology doesn't in fact name an autonomous condition of possibility but rather a reinscription of the Humanist paradigm of "civilisation" by other means. If the avantgarde's "transgression" of the systematicity of this paradigm is not, as Bataille argues, an "access to the immediate & indeterminate *identity* of a non-meaning," this is because its operations themselves derive from that *alienation* at the origin of the very conception of the system, of work, of productivity, & consequently of recuperation, institutionalisation, totalisation.

It is at the point at which the reinscription of this paradigm *fails* that the function of the avantgarde comes into view not simply as critique or subversion but as an *excess of production*: not in the form of a surplus-value, but of a *compulsive dissipation* that invests the principle of value itself from its inception & tends to exponential increase. Consequently, the work of the avantgarde can be regarded as a *discourse of the irrecuperable*, born of the "impoverishment" of totality as it succumbs to the entropic labour required to sustain the illusion of itself. This irrecuperability is the nondeductable element of art-work itself, regardless of the subsequent institutional trajectories of the socalled *artwork*, within the historical confines of an avantgard*ism*. In this, the failure of totalisation – as it slides towards the "loss of sense" at its horizon – is always to some extent an "aesthetics" of the sublime, in which the old ontological unity of History & method, envisaged by Hegel, is reduced to that parodic cybernetic conundrum that presents itself in Bataille in the form of the question, "Who will ever know what it is to know nothing?"[92]

---

[92] Bataille, "Le Petit," *Louis XXX*, trans. Stewart Kendall (London: Equus Press, 2013) 23.

REALISM'S ANTIPODE

> Modernity must be under the sign of suicide,
> an act which seals an heroic will…
> – Walter Benjamin, *Charles Baudellaire*

The 1937 *Entartete "Kunst"* ("Degenerate 'Art'") exhibition – of over 650 paintings, sculptures, prints & books, staged by the Nazis at the former Munich Institute of Archaeology for the purpose of enlightening the German populace to the evils of socalled modern art – featured an intentionally chaotic array of work by children, psychiatric patients & artists ranging from Van Gogh to Chagall, but held a particular place of contempt for the German Dadaists & Surrealists: George Grosz, Raoul Hausmann, Hans Richter, Rudolf Schlichter, Kurt Schwitters & Max Ernst. The exhibition served as the prelude to later spectacles of mass vandalism, like the bonfire – staged in the gardens of the Galerie nationale de Jeu de Paume in Paris, on July 27, 1942 – of works by Picasso, Dalí, Klee, Léger, Miró & Ernst. The *Entartete "Kunst"* catalogue denounced the "specific intellectual ideal" of modern art as that of "the idiot, the cretin, & the cripple" & present "the Negro & the South Sea Islander" as its "evident racial ideal." At the 1935 Nuremburg rally, Hitler himself proclaimed, "It isn't the mission of art to wallow in filth for filth's sake, to paint the human being only in a state of putrefaction, to draw cretins as symbols of motherhood, or to present deformed idiots as representatives of manly strength."

The aggressive "primitivism" & "anti-rationalism" of Dada & Surrealism, with their unrelenting attacks on precisely the corrupted mythos & cultural "logic" that constituted National-Socialist ideology, was summed up by the organizers of *Entartete "Kunst"* (un-ironically, of course) as "madness becomes method." Drawing from Dada's assault upon the mercantile-imperialist global order that produced WWI & the jingoistic nationalisms that proliferated after Versailles, Surrealism in particular set itself the task of a social transformation on the order of collective consciousness, through a revival of the revolutionary "spirit" of the 1870s & Rimbaud's "systematic disordering of the senses." As a polemic, Surrealism positioned itself as the adversary of a totalizing Rationalism: a Rationalism that it perceived as fundamentally *irrational* at its core, like Goya's "slumber of reason" whose engendered monsters were not those works of "Entartete Kunst" denounced by the Nazis, but the very impulse to denunciation – an impulse already manifested & institutionalized far beyond the borders & racialist policies of the Third Reich.

Announced in the 1924 "Manifesto of Surrealism," this "anti-rational" programme of social transformation, as conceived by its most active proponent, André Breton, was one of a profound *disillusionment*. "So strong is the belief in life," wrote Breton in the Manifesto's opening line, "in what is most fragile in life – *real* life, I mean – that in the end this belief is lost." Life, the Surrealist's insisted, had been done to death by socalled realism, & by those paragons of "rationality" & "enlightenment" whose ultimate contribution to humanity was the machinery of global oppression, world war & genocide. While subsequently the path of humanity's emancipation from this deathly "realism" would be seen to lie along the path of political transformation opened up by the Bolshevik revolution (however fraught their interpretation of this would turn out to be), the principle concern of the Surrealists was with the emancipation of mind (of "man, that inveterate dreamer") & the liberation of art from the dictates of ideology: a *de facto* principle of "revolution" that would achieve its clearest formulation in the collaborative 1938 manifesto, co-authored by Breton & Trotsky, "For an Independent Revolutionary Art."[1]

While the guiding impulse of Breton's programme stemmed from the psychoanalytic writings of Freud & Breton's own field hospital work during WWI, the principle methodology of Surrealism – what ultimately set it apart from a mere theoretical prospectus – stemmed from a revived understanding of poetics (indeed, this is the point both Freud & Breton had most in common, since it is necessary to regard Freud's seminal work, *Die Traumdeutung*, as an investigation of the *poetics* of dream logic, & ultimately of consciousness itself). Midway through the 1924 manifesto, Breton famously defined Surrealism as "psychic automatism in its pure state, by which one proposes to express – verbally, by means of the written word, or in any other manner – the actual functioning of thought."[2] This *actual functioning of thought* was expressed, moreover, as "an absence of any *control* exercised by reason" & "exempt from any *ethical or moral concern*."

---

[1] To deflect from the controversy surrounding Trotsky, the manifesto was in fact co-signed by Breton & Trotsky's Mexican host, Diego Rivera, though Rivera unsurprisingly played no discernible part in its composition.

[2] André Breton, "Manifesto of Surrealism," *Manifestoes of Surrealism*, trans. Richard Seaver & Helen R. Lane (Ann Arbor: University of Michigan Press, 1969) 26.

In other words, the truth of Surrealism was to be located not within a given ideological standpoint, or programme of instruction, but the contrary: a radical ambivalence. *Not an ambivalence towards any ethics whatsoever*, for example, but rather the *ambivalence of thought itself, in its formation,* which would be a mark of its autonomy from ethical preconceptions, or of any system of intellectual coercion; an *emancipated thought* – on the basis of which *an ethics could be founded.* This in itself was a radical position that was quickly mischaracterised as one of gratuitous irresponsibility – much in the manner of Dada, but more dangerous for its appeal to subjective as well as collective experience &, through the Bureau for Surrealist Research, for its quasi-systematic grounding in a kind of scientism. Like the spectre of Marxism, Surrealism aspired not to a merely nihilistic "critique," but to become the means of real social transformation.

Realism à l'envers

The 1924 Manifesto came ready-packed with practical applications of the idea of "pure psychic automatism." These in themselves were important for indicating an aesthetic path, but more important was the construction of method – & this method in turn drew its force from an insight into the logic of poetic construction: an insight that would have universal applicability & which, in addition to the prestige & narcissistic appeal of the dream lives of others, would account for the movement's rapid international spread, particularly among those for whom psychic *repression* & political *oppression* were synonymous, & for whom social realism presented a visible incommensurability with lived experience. And it's here that we might speak of a certain *antipodeanism* brought into view by the Surrealist project: the world *underfoot*, the *inverse*, *upsidedown* dimension of the real that isn't a *mirror* of representation but representation's *underworld*. Its *envers*. Its *enfer*. A radical antipodeanism of language, of mind, & indeed of all ideological systems of collective & individual control, exploitation & colonialisation. An antipodeanism which, aroused to consciousness, might become – like Marx's downtrodden – a critical, emancipative force. Realism's proletariat.

This revolutionary aspect of Surrealism stems precisely from the question of representation. Surrealism, with its particular purview on the world & upon the ideology of realism, was concerned with the status of representation as such: both of this antipodean *surreality* &

of Surrealist praxis itself. Confronted at the outset with the quandary of the *unpresentable*, but persuaded in the belief that not only did the unpresentable *exist* but that it constituted *the very basis of reality*, Breton reversed Freud's analysis of the *semiotic* character of dreams into a poetic methodology, for which he discovered antecedents in the writings of Pierre Reverdy firstly & later (& more persuasively) in those of Lautréamont.

Midway through the 1924 manifesto, Breton quotes from a text by Reverdy published at the end of WWI: "The image," Reverdy wrote, "is a pure creation of the mind. / It cannot be born from a comparison but from a juxtaposition of two more or less distant realities. / The more distant & true, the stronger the image will be – the greater its emotional power & poetic reality…" In 1925 a special issue of the Surrealist magazine *Le Disque Vert* was dedicated to Lautréamont, who was born in Uruguay & died in 1870 at the age of 24, & whose description of a young boy in *Les Chants de Maldoror* as "beautiful as the chance encounter on a dissection table of a sewing-machine & an umbrella," became a sort of operating-manual in miniature for the technique of Surrealist collage[3] – exemplified early on by the *exquisite corpse*, & later reprised in what Dalí would characterize as a *critical paranoiac method*, & Guy Debord (anchored in the critical praxis of John Heartfield) would refine into *détournement*, as a putting to work of radical incommensurabilities to produce an unforeseen re-ordering of sense & of the constitution of the "real." A technique, in other words, of accessing the unpresentable through the violent (if temporary) overthrow of the ideology of representation itself.

One of the most fluent practitioners of the technique of Surrealist collage, however, was Max Ernst. Co-founder with Hans Arp & Johannes Baargeld of the Cologne-based Zentrale W/3, Ernst had made a name for himself as the instigator of the 1919 *Dada-Vorfrüling* ("Dada Spring") exhibition, entered via a men's urinal in which a woman in a communion dress recited obscene poetry. Viewers were invited to destroy the works on show (including Baargeld's *Anthropophiliac Tapeworm* & Ernst's *Original Running Frieze from the Lung of a Seventeen-Year-Old Smoker*), with hammers provided for that purpose. Despite this propensity to auto-critique, the exhibition was closed down by police due to public outrage ("fraud," "obscenity," "creating a public scandal"). Its immediate effect was to gain Ernst an invitation from Breton to stage an exhibition in Paris.

---

[3] Encompassing Dadaist photomontage, as well as Soviet film-montage & *litmontaz*.

Ernst described his work of this period as *sculpto-peinture* – like Schwitter's "Merz," an assemblage of found material arranged more or less at random. He defined his technique, echoing Lautréamont, as "the systematic exploitation of the fortuitous or engineered encounter of two or more intrinsically incompatible realities on a surface which is manifestly inappropriate for the purpose – & the spark of poetry which leaps across the gap as these two realities are brought together."[4] It was at this time that Ernst began producing collages drawn from 19th-century book illustrations (woodcuts, line blocks, steel engravings), an activity that would form the basis of two of his best-known later serial compositions, *La Femme 100 têtes* (1929) & *Une semaine de bonté* (1934) – described as "pictorial novels."

La Femme 100 têtes, consisting of 147 prints, appeared with a forward by Breton, while Ernst himself offered that the particular intensity of the collages "derives as much from the emotional commonplaces which serve as their point of departure as from the uses – no less sacrilegious, one could say, than purely absurd – to which they are put."[5] *Une semaine de bonté*, published in five volumes, drew among others on the illustrational work of Gustave Doré (the principle source of Ernst's bird-headed figures), détourning what has been described as Victorian visual platitudes into bizarrely unsettling manifestations of unconscious sociopathic intent – thereby transforming banal advertisements for a bourgeois world-view into melodramas of prohibited desire. Uwe Schneede describes Ernst as handling his material "with great mastery, like a scientific observer... & setting out, like Freud, to demonstrate the effects of sexual repression in human life":

> It is for this very reason that these collages have such extreme suggestive power: they derive their impact not from the formal interplay of pictorial elements, but from the analysis of social realities.[6]

---

[4] Qtd in Uwe M. Schneede, *The Essential Max Ernst*, trans. R.W. Last (London: Thames & Hudson, 1972) 29.

[5] Qtd from John Russell, *Max Ernst: Life & Work* (London: Thames & Hudson, 1967), in Schneede, *The Essential Max Ernst*, 112.

[6] Schneede, *The Essential Max Ernst*, 139.

The Disappearances of Civilisation

Bella Li's *Argosy*, published in Sydney in 2017, explicitly reversions Ernst's collage novels in a work of Surrealist antipodeanism *après la letter* that poses questions about the contemporary critical impetus of a poetics of collage.[7] Li's book, comprised of pictorial collage sequences & sequences of dreamlike "poetic prose" or "prose poems," divides equally into two sections: "Pérouse, ou, Une semaine de disparitions" (alluding to the scientific expedition of the Compte de La Pérouse, which vanished in 1788 in the South Pacific) & "The Hundred Headless Woman." By way of these advertisements, *Argosy* invites reading as a détournement of a détournement. In the collage sequences of "Pérouse," Ernst's bird-headed & bat-winged Victorians are transmuted into bird-headed colonial officers, giant "South Sea Islanders," animal-vegetable-insect hybrids, ships rigged with nautilus shells, bizarre Lepidoptera, & other suchlike cropped from tinted 18th & 19th-century etchings. Freudian perversion among the European bourgeoisie gives way to an ethno-anthropology of the fantastically "other."

"Pérouse, ou, Une semaine de disparitions" is a pictorial voyage that draws from a mix of exotica & scientific record (the distinctions between which are frequently ambivalent in any case), evoking – among other things – ideas of the Enlightenment "noble savage" whose cretinised doppelgangers came to haunt the Nazi evangelists of *Entartete "Kunst."* The disappearance of the expedition of La Pérouse after it had set sail from Botany Bay & its brief encounter with Arthur Philip's "first fleet" (sent by the British admiralty to colonise New South Wales), hovers in the background like an unsettling premonition of the European "civilising project" of which Li's source material was the pictorial embellishment. It eventually came to be believed that La Pérouse's shipwrecked crew had been "massacred" by "natives" on the island of Vanikoro.

But we may suspect that, beyond this implication of "irrational menace" (one which serves to obscure, of course, the *disappearance* of indigenous cultures in the Pacific & elsewhere in the wake of such voyages of European Enlightenment – just as in Perec's *La Disparition*, for example, it's the internal *disappearance* of Europe's Jews in the wake of Nazi "Enlightenment"), there is another, immeasurably more frivolous "disappearance" being alluded to in Li's book: that of the Surrealist poet Paul Éluard. Éluard, whose writings ghost the textual sequences of

[7] Bella Li, *Argosy* (Sydney: Vagabond, 2017).

Argosy, notoriously staged a mysterious vanishing act from Paris in 1925, which turned out (to Breton's intense disgust) to be a rich man's "round-the-world" holiday cruise, whose itinerary – Marseilles, Gaudeloupe, Martinique, Panama, Tahiti, Cook Islands, Wellington, Sydney, Brisbane, the Dutch East Indies, Singapore (where he rendezvoused with Max Ernst), Saigon, Colombo, Djibouti, Suez, Marseilles – was the stuff of postcards & literary travelogue. La Pérouse of the interwar art-tourist class, with a picturesque nod to Gauguin, pared of any threat from local "savages" (though syphilis, the pre-eminent European disease, yes). Breton's disgust, it ought to be remembered, stemmed not from Éluard's snobbism but from the sheer *banality* of his "voyage": its betrayal of Surrealist mythos.

By contrast, the sequences in Li's *Argosy* that comprise "Hundred Headless Woman" are concerned with a different genre of disappearance: that, within the main body of (predominantly male) Surrealist art, of "woman" into fetish ("the true, captivating stereotypy"[8]) – of which attitude Breton's *Nadja* represented the very apotheoses. Despite its referencing of Ernst, "Hundred Headless Woman" is predominantly textual ("Isidora: A Western," "The Novelist Elena Ferrante," "The Memory Machine Elena Obieta"), the sole collage sequence ("Eve & Co.") being made up of hand-drawn figures cut from 1950s dressmaking magazines & pasted into contemporary North American streetscapes. The terrain is one of a more *implicit* détournement of the representation of gender. In conjunction with the examination of ethno-exoticism in "Pérouse," "Hundred Headless Woman" thereby touches upon a larger recurring element in Surrealist antipodeanism, which is that of the conflation of the "feminine" & the "primitive" as tropes of a seductive/emancipative *irrationalism* to be ranged against the morbidity of European "civilisation" *à la mode*.

And here lies another problem. For while the techniques of Surrealist collage avail themselves of what, at a given moment, represent a revolt against stereotype, moral hypocrisy, & so on – exposing latent contradictions while suggesting whole worlds of "unpresentable" experience – they equally avail themselves of the contrary. It was precisely the *fluency* of Ernst's collage-novels in the first place – like that of Dalí & Picasso – which bred imitators on a quasi-industrial scale, & through this work of "imitation" (& in the case of Dalí & Picasso,

---

[8] André Breton, *Point du jour* (Paris: Gallimard, 1934) 233.

self-parody) produced a "tendency to evoke superficially"[9] resulting in the domestication of Surrealism as *style*. We move, in a manner indistinguishable from commodification, from Surrealism's bounty to its poverty. And just as Surrealist "method" is reducible to style, so is its critique – but here's the rub: insofar as Breton founded a *method* upon a clear analysis of a poetics – indeed of a mechanism of construction, one which (by its very *ambivalence* to its terms) is universalisable – so too the logic of "Surrealist" critique is founded upon the generalisation of "critical logic" as such. Its subversion thus requires the surrender of all essentialisms: beyond Surrealism there is only naked commodities.

Revolutionary Surrealism

In one of the sections of *La Société du spectacle* concerned with "spectacular consumption," Debord notes that, "The two currents that marked the end of modern art were Dadaism & surrealism." "Historically," he adds, "Dadaism & surrealism are at once bound up with one another & at odds with one another… For Dadaism sought to *abolish art without realising it* & surrealism sought to *realise art without abolishing it."*[10]

Debord's 1957 "Report on the Construction of Situations" had already identified the sentimental "return of Surrealism" as specifically a "return to art": that is to say, to the *institution of art*. Co-opted "into ordinary aesthetic commerce," what was once transgressive in Surrealism isn't merely domesticated & neutralised, but cultivated "as a sort of nostalgia" (i.e. for the radicalism *of the past* preserved "in a congealed form") which henceforth "discredits any new venture." It is only, in other words, in the normalisation of Surrealism *as art* (which it embraced in any case), that its radicalism is permitted to be acknowledged, & acknowledged moreover as *definitive* (the "most disturbing movement possible"), thus neutralising not only what was most radical about Surrealist critique, but disarming in its name any future critique (which can only be regarded as a pale imitation, etc.).[11] "The most extreme destruction," Debord argues,

---

[9] Breton, *Point du jour*, 234.

[10] Guy Debord, *The Society of the Spectacle*, trans. Donald Nicholson Smith (New York: Zone, 1995) §191.

[11] Guy Debord, "Report in the Construction of Situations & on the Internationalist Situationist Tendency's Condition of Organization & Action," *Situationist International Anthology*, ed. & trans. Ken Knabb (Berkeley: Bureau of Public Secrets, 1981) 19.

can be officially welcomed as a positive development because it amounts to yet one more way of flaunting one's acceptance of a status quo where all communication has been smugly declared absent.[12]

In his 1935 Prague lecture on "The Surrealist Situation of the Object (Situation of the Surrealist Object)," Breton himself stated that "the greatest danger threatening Surrealism today is the fact that because of its spread throughout the world, which was very sudden & rapid, the word found favour much faster than the idea & all sorts of more or less questionable creations tend to pin the Surrealist label on themselves." To avoid misunderstandings of this kind, which stem from a certain fetishisation & a certain cultishness, Breton proposed the following:

> The best way to seek agreement on this question seems to me to seek to determine the exact situation of the Surrealist object today. This situation is of course the correlative of another, the Surrealist situation of the object. It is only when we have reached perfect agreement on the way in which Surrealism represents the object in general – this table, the photograph that that man over there has in his pocket, a tree at the very instant that it is struck by lightning, an aurora borealis, or, to enter the domain of the impossible, a flying lion – that there can arise the question of defining the place that the Surrealist object must take to justify the adjective Surrealist.[13]

It is unavoidable, however, to recognise that the Surrealist "situation" – as with the situation of Surrealist collage (& of montage in general) – is precariously relative: its underlying ambivalence *cuts both ways*. The very possibility of a *sur*-realism demands it: its critical impetus can never be conflated with an essential "Surrealism" of any kind, because its very contingency, its very *force*, leaves it open to precisely the same movement by which it initiates itself. In other words, what "justifies" the adjective Surrealist isn't any kind of *object*, & least of all an aesthetic artefact, but its *displacement* – or, as Li puts it, its "disappearance." If Ernst's *La Femme 100 têtes* & *Une semaine de bonté* imply a certain "disappearance" of one European idea, Li's channelling of Ernst in "Pérouse, ou, Une semaine de disparitions" & "The Hundred Headless Woman" implies another: an idea bound to the situation *of the "Surrealist" subject*.

---

[12] Debord, *The Society of the Spectacle*, §192.
[13] André Breton, "The Surrealist Situation of the Object (Situation of the Surrealist Object)," *Manifestoes of Surrealism*, 258.

Take for example Tzara's 1918 "Note sur la poésie nègre," in which he notes: "we are God only for the country of our knowledge, in the laws according to which we live our experience on this Earth, on both sides of our equator, inside our borders."[14] Tzara's anthropoetics – one of the unacknowledged impetuses of early Surrealism – poses the question of critical *frames of reference* in terms of the problem of universality: can a universal situation of "poetry" be brought into view, unless through a projection or displacement into otherness? This problem is almost immediately confused with that of the "origins" of the poetic impulse, as an anthropological condition, & the consequent appeal of an aesthetic "primitivism." The risk here is that Tzara's implied question, once inverted, would appear to cause an entire epistemological rationale to disappear: just as Li's work implies (through a repositioning of the Surrealist frames of reference around an antipodal & feminist subjectivity) a spectrology of Surrealism that also marks its definitive "disappearance."

Myth of the Indigène

Tzara's "translation" of socalled *negro* poetry – which begins with "The Kangaroo," sourced from "Luritcha (North Australia)" – is really a method of *détournement*: situating what we might call the quasi-Surrealist object within a field of collage called European culture. And while it is necessary to speak of the hegemonic character of such ethnological "translations," it is also necessary to acknowledge the very contingent, indeed ambivalent character of their orientation. For just as translation plays upon a representation of the unpresentable (or *representation as disappearance*), it also poses a threat: the instant the "object" translates into a "subject," the direction of disappearance is reversed. There is, within Surrealism, an element of hysteria, to possess its object so as not to be obliterated by it – such that the only thing guarding it becomes, like Ernst's prolific output, an inflationary manufacture of *situations*.

The force of collage's *radical ambivalence* (what Breton called "the triumph of the equivocal"[15]) consequently returns, like Marx's tragedy sublimated into farce, in the *necessary ramification* of precisely the formulaic, in the manufacture of new stereotypes, new pictorial conventions, in a whole *stylistics* (the "poverty," in Breton's words, of a "poetry" that, brought to an impasse, dies of itself, of inertia, of

[14] Tristan Tzara, "A Note on Negro Poetry," trans. Pierre Joris, *4x1* (Albany: Inconundrum, 2002) 15.
[15] Breton, *Point du jour*, 236.

boredom). Necessary, because on the one hand the assumption of *any* critical POV implies a *reductio ad absurdum* (the open-ended critique-of-critique), & because on the other – in revealing the arbitrary construction of supposed essentialisms – it presents itself as a method for aesthetically reconciling precisely the contradictions it exposes. "We now know," Debord writes, "that the unconscious imagination is poor, that automatic writing is monotonous, and that the whole genre of ostentatious surrealist "weirdness" has ceased to be very surprising. The formal fidelity to this style of imagination ultimately leads back to *the antipodes of the modern conditions of imagination*: back to traditional occultism."[16] Or as Bataille puts it, "All claims from below have been surreptitiously disguised as claims from above."

This is the terrain – mediated by the intervening discourse of postmodernism – which Li's *Argosy* traverses, so to speak, in its evocation of a "return of the spectre of Surrealism" as a "return of Surrealism's repressed" – concluding with what can only be described as a simulacrum of a Sam Taylor-Wood art-fashion shoot, featuring a faceless (female) model posed in a series of locations *à la mode*, entitled "La ténébreuse" (French, because it's about as "exotic" as a perfume label, while the shadowy *other* is always "foreign"). There is a deep ambivalence here, between the economy of a "return to the origin" as avant-primitivism & as fundamentalist reaction, in which the *antipodean* describes a paradigmatic movement. This can be summed up in the somewhat paradoxical observation that, "As for the productions of peoples who are still subject to cultural colonialism (often caused by political oppression), even though they may be progressive in their own countries, they play a reactionary role in advanced cultural countries."[17]

It's in this respect, also, that Debord speaks of Surrealism as leading "back to traditional occultism," a summoning of *dark powers* (the force of the unpresentable) no longer in the service of revelation but as a bulwark *against disappearance*. In China Miéville's 2016 novel, *The Last Days of New Paris*,[18] the spectre of Surrealism is rendered in vastly threatening & paradoxical terms of *resistance*. Miéville's novel "recuperates" the Surrealist antipodeanism that frames Li's détournements back onto the figure of the

---

[16] Debord, "Report in the Construction of Situations & on the Internationalist Situationist Tendancy's Condition of Organization & Action," 19 – emphasis added.

[17] Guy Debord, "The Role of Minority Tendencies in the Ebbing Period," *Situationist International Anthology*, 20.

[18] China Miéville, *The Last Days of New Paris* (London: Picador, 2016).

Surrealist "capital": Paris. The novel is topologically situated in a zone of psychic quarantine, between the 1941 Surrealist exodus in the face of Nazi occupation & the fictional endgame of a WWII situated in an alternative "Surrealist" history: in "1950."[19] Miéville's war is one in which the French Surrealist *résistance* group – "La main à plume" – are caught in a battle between occultist Nazis & rampaging "manifestations" let loose from the collective unconscious by a reality-altering "S-blast" (a massive Surrealist neuron bomb).

The S–Blast

The historical Main-à-Plume was a Surrealist derivation active under the Occupation from 1941-1944 (during which time Breton & company were absent from Paris, in exile in New York), led by Robert Ruis, Jean Simonpoli & Marco Ménégoz. Their group-name referred to a line from Rimbaud, "La main à plume vaut la main à charrue," in *Une Saison en enfer*. In June 1944 they formed a *maquis*, which operated in the Fontainbleu forest, until the group was betrayed a month later & its members were imprisoned, tortured & shot (but only after refusing to talk). The theme of betrayal in *The Last Days of New Paris* is closely linked here to an allegory of art at the service of ideology & the recurring theme of failed revolution, not least of which is *la révolution surréaliste* (where the silence of the historical Main-à-Plume stands in notable contrast to Miéville's "confessional" fictionalisation).

Miéville's novel centres upon a 3-way drama around his fictional Main-à-Plume's last surviving member, "Thibault" – who possesses an uncanny affinity with Surrealist objects ("manifs") – Jack Parsons, a real-life occultist & rocket scientist (acolyte of the "Great Beast," Aleister Crowley), & "Sam," a kind of one-woman analogue of Operation Paperclip & the Manhattan Project. Miéville's Paris is accordingly a kind of Paris upsidedown, an antipodean Paris, *à l'envers* or rather *à l'enfer*: a portal of hell, of that Terra Australis Incognita of the European imaginary, situated somewhere between Mororua Atoll (the site of French Pacific nuclear weapons testing between 1966 & 1996) & Les Deux Magots.

---

[19] A first-person postscript brings us up to the recent present, in which Miéville mimes himself (in a set-piece of the genre) as the unexpected recipient of the foregoing "account" from the mouth of an aged, unidentified "witness." He's merely the conduit, in the public interest, of a story he can neither verify nor disprove (were he inclined to do either): the "writer," we are led to understand, is *historically impotent* in the face of contested realisms.

At the heart of this novel is a proposition, which harks back to the premises of *Entartete "Kunst"* & bears out, in a deeply ambivalent form, the prospect of Surrealist social transformation as a chaos of unreason. Where Li's project evokes a decorous mannerism as the camouflage of counter-critique, Miéville's evokes a gamespace of rampaging "exquisite corpses" & demons as allegory of the ideological capture of "no future." Here, the reifications of perpetual Surrealism stand as counterparts to a Fukuyamaesque neoliberal "end of history," in which revolt & resistance are reduced to videogame parlour décor of commodified dissent.

Two dates, then: 1941, 1950. These are the historical co-ordinates of Miéville's dialectic of the "Last Man": resistance fighter, fantasist, writer. His account begins, non-chronologically, in 1950: something arrives out of a hostile & improbable distance, assuming a form at once concrete & phantasmagoric: it is Leonora Carrington's 1941 pen-&-ink work, *I am an Amateur of Velocipedes* – a female oracle of sorts, tasked with delivering three messages, one spoken, one written, one in the form of a Surrealist playing card. The mysterium of plot: messages from the past convoking a future for a quasi-fictive world in which otherwise there is none. Close the book, 12 February 1950, real world (socalled): Albert Einstein raises the spectre of Mutually Assured Destruction resulting from any nuclear war. Assuredly, M.A.D. saturates Miéville's novel, like some overwhelming background radiation bleeding through the protective fictional membrane in which New Paris is quarantined from "reality." Rewind to January 24, the elided subplot of a distended war against Nazi Germany & the occupation of Paris: in a prelude to the Rosenberg trial, nuclear physicist Klaus Fuchs confesses under interrogation by MI5 to being a Soviet spy – for seven years he's passed secret data on British & US atomic weapons research to Moscow. In Miéville's novel, the Soviet Union & the Cold War arms race will remain the elephant in the room.

Rewind to 1949, 29 August, Semipalatinsk, Kazakhstan: the Soviets conduct their first successful weapons test, codenamed First Lightning – in response, Truman orders the rapid development of a hydrogen bomb, initiating a race that will culminate in the Soviet Union's detonation of the "Tsar Bomba" – producing the largest yield ever recorded, an estimated 50 - 58 megatons – on Severny Island in the Arctic Ocean, 30 October 1961. To illustrate the bomb's destructive potential on a major urban centre, & to galvanise the European public, a diagram is disseminated of the bomb's 60 mile blast radius superimposed on a map of the Île de France region, with Paris at its epicentre. The message is clear: in one fell stroke, the "Tsar Bomba" would be capable *in fact* of doing to Old Paris what Le Corbusier's 1925 "Plan Voisin" for the construction of a "New Paris" had, in an act of grandiose *symbolical* provocation, merely dreamt of. (Announcing his project to demolish the 3rd & 4th arrondissements upon which to erect a new modernist city, Le Corbusier proclaimed, "At the present moment a congress on 'The New Paris' is about to assemble... Paris of tomorrow could be magnificently equal to the march of events that is day by day bringing us ever nearer to the dawn of a new social contract.") It would represent, in fact, a type of ideal disappearance – *of the very idea of Paris*. In its presentation of the unpresentable, the *rationality* of the bomb would effectively bring the "European" project of "civilisation" full circle, from auto-critique to suicide.

Here, as elsewhere, historical detail provides an alibi for realism's (reason's) imminent betrayal: such betrayal will provide the appreciable subtext of Miéville's novel, yet its agency will not be that of the Axis Powers or those of the Cold War, but Surrealism itself. In unleashing the forces of radical ambivalence, Miéville appears to argue that the Surrealists confected not only their own disappearance, but that of the very revolutionary possibility they advanced upon the world. As if to say, in fact, that the germ of neoliberalism – of global commodification & its discontents – lay not in the cynical expropriation of Surrealist technique, etc., but in the very *logic* of Surrealism, its occult mechanics, the *mythos* of the S-blast, in which the "dark powers" of the global order – from *Tausendjähriges Reich* to the *New American Century* – manifest as pure phantasmagoria.

LITERATURE'S INCEST MACHINES

> He proves by algebra that Hamlet's grandson is Shakespeare's grandfather
> & that he himself is the ghost of his own father.
> – James Joyce, *Ulysses*

Richard Ellmann famously opened his biography of Joyce with the words, "We are still learning to be James Joyce's contemporaries, to understand our interpreter."[1] But is that as true today as it apparently was when Ellmann wrote it in 1959? And what of that seeming contrary movement, absent here, of a "Joyce" who becomes *our* contemporary – just as, in *Ulysses*, Stephen Dedalus insists, by algebra or otherwise, on a "Shakespeare" who is *his* contemporary, & not some erected piety?

In the Winter 1977 issue of *TriQuarterly* magazine – one of the few remaining magazines in America at that time with a specific purview on experimentalism & the avantgarde (now all but defunct) – David Hayman, guest-editing a survey of contemporary writing "in the wake of the *Wake*" (including work by Augusto de Campos, Maurice Roche, Hélène Cixous, Philippe Sollers, Arno Schmidt, Christine-Brooke-Rose, Samuel Beckett, Raymond Federman, John Cage, Gilbert Sorentino & William Gass) duly noted that "for a *growing number* of writers of 'experimental' fiction… Joyce's *Wake* must be a prime exemplar."[2]

Hayman's stance came ten years after William Burroughs – frequently regarded as a major protagonist of the post-War experimental "movement" – replied in an interview to the claim that "*Finnegans Wake* is generally regarded as a magnificent literary dead end," by saying, "*Finnegans Wake* rather represents a trap into which experimental writing can fall when it becomes *purely experimental*."[3] Burroughs's point speaks not only to an industry-sponsored view that "Modernism" had exhausted itself with Joyce & required a "call to order," but to the question that arises in both Ellmann's & Hayman's figuring of Joyce as effectively a prescription for the "contemporary," or of the "experimental," as a "one-way street" – wherein both of these terms do less to reflect an open engagement with Joyce than to expose the posthumous character of a certain "neo-Joyceanism."

---

[1] Richard Ellman, *James Joyce* (London: Faber & Faber, 1959) 1.
[2] David Hayman, "Some writers in the wake of the *Wake*," *TriQuarterly* 38 (Winter 1977): 1 – emphasis added.
[3] William S. Burroughs and Daniel Didier, "Journey through time-space," *The Job* (New York: Evergreen, 1974) 55 – emphasis added.

Revenant Textual Cybernetics

Eighty years after the publication of the *Wake*, what future is there for socalled experimental writing? And what place does Joyce hold in that future? Which is to say, a future as perceived from the vantage of Ellman & Hayman, arraigned in full view of that looking glass of its own effecting, with its spectres dutifully gathered behind it. A very "Joycean" vantage. The vantage of the nursery playpen or the monastic typing pool: of the future in need of a Father & of the Word authentically transmitted. The vantage of a certain pedagogy, of learning to be Joyce's contemporary; of learning to write in the wake of the *Wake*.

Of course, there's more to Ellmann's & Hayman's remarks than such an implied pedantry, but not always. This is the risk of any messianism. In the case of Joyce, there has been the tendency to conflate in him the messianism of avantgardes in general, so that in his neo-manifestations Joyce has frequently become the paradigm of a certain post-literary avantgardism itself, married to precisely that kind of textual paternalism Joyce himself did so much to disrupt; which is to say, of that curious paradox arising from an impatience with the past & an Oedipal attachment to its own belatedness.

Concerning Joyce, there are two points that need to be acknowledged from the outset. The first being that Joyce himself was never a participant in any avantgarde movement, his stance toward the avantgarde having always been one of a rather self-serving scepticism, all things considered. This has in no way prevented Joyce, however, from coming to represent something of an apotheosis of the historical avantgarde "project." The second being that, in tandem with this apotheosis – which is also to say, institutionalization & thereby neutralization – the Joyce "brand" has increasingly come to stand for, & to be an active & substantial agent within, a dominant post-War cultural capitalism. In this respect, we might say that Adorno's "culture industry" *is* the neo-avantgarde whose predominance Peter Bürger has so strenuously lamented, while "Joyce" has duly been erected as one of that industry's temporal idols (& sub-franchised to a whole array of "post-literatures," from Felix Guattari's *Chaosophy*, to Mark Amerika's *Grammatron*, Mark Danielewski's *The Familiar* & Derek Beaulieu's neo-conceptualist Wakean contour drawings). This state of affairs has come about precisely by way of the implied interdiction that insists we learn to become "Joyce's contemporaries" without Joyce ever being permitted to be claimed as ours. The more radical gesture than Hayman's wake-ism (in the spirit of Burroughs; notably absent from

Hayman's anthology) is to refuse all such permissions & steal into the Temple past the merchandising stands – plaster-of-Paris Jimbos & all that – make a grab at the Scriptures, then get out fast before the rent-a-cops & Philistines storm the exits.

There's a curious episode toward the end of the "antinovel" *Downriver* by Iain Sinclair where the author provides us with a portrait, so to speak, of what this play of Joycean contemporeneity might look like when it admits the paternalism & Oedipal violence that necessarily comes with it. *Downriver* traverses the riverine of *Finnegans Wake*'s parallel city, London, whose literary "recuperation" by way of an "occultist psychogeography" represents a singular preoccupation for Sinclair, whose complete bibliography may in turn be considered a unified Gesamtkunstwerk in this respect – just as Joyce's *Wake* is taken to represent a type of universal history in holograph. But such a parallel isn't arbitrary, for whilst Sinclair is not an outward emulator of the later Joyce (such as we find among Hayman's wakeists), there is from the outset of Sinclair's project something of Jacob wrestling with the angel atop that middenheap of filth that, Ararat-like, surmounts the primal soup of language from which History slithers forth toward its Bethlehem – in the guise, perhaps, of some latter-day Anthony Burgess. For Joyce is a kind of persistent if frequently unacknowledged demon in the occult world of Sinclair (who was born a year after Joyce's death).

Let us picture the ghost of Joyce, blind as a bat, accompanying Sinclair on his psychogeographic pilgrimages along the Thames – as once he'd accompanied Nora Barnacle to a London registry office sixty years before, a displaced, itinerant genius loci, a spiritual Gastarbeiter groping about among the "countrymen of Ben Jonson," in the shadow of whose language his alterego's "soul frets."[4] It's there, at the end of this millennial journey, toward a proverbial daybreak that echoes the concluding passages of *Heart of Darkness* (Joyce's Dublin & Conrad's Belgian Congo brought into sudden confluence), that an epigraph appears, drawn from the last page of *Finnegans Wake*: "I see them rising! Save me from those therrble prongs!"[5] which takes on wondrously sinister connotations as the Liffy flows back, "saltsick," into the arms of her "cold mad feary father," etc.

And it's at precisely this moment, at what we might call the Joyce nexus of his project, that Sinclair-as-narrator addresses a letter to his other erstwhile companion – disguised in the figure of one S.L. Joblard

[4] James Joyce, *A Portrait of the Artist as a Young Man* (New York: Viking Press, 1966) 189.
[5] James Joyce, *Finnegans Wake* (London: Faber & Faber, 1939) 628.4-5.

("the French for 'ninny,' 'simpleton'"; avatar of the sculptor Brian Catling, author of *The Vorrh* [2012], it so happens). Joblard appears & reappears with some frequency throughout Sinclair's writing, evoking the notion that "when two men meet a third is always present"[6] (a case, perhaps, of the left hand not knowing whose plume the right hand is holding), implying, among other things, a kind of Joycean three-body-problem of not-quite "consubstantial" alteregos. It is in effect like Lear's opening speech, a letter of abdication, of Sinclair's "need to write himself out of his own story," as one critic has it,[7] insisting that Joblard finish the work on his behalf; his executor, his proxy:

> Either you (S.L. Joblard) become "I," or the story ends here. In petulant recrimination. I & I can only wish you luck.
>   Sincerely, S[8]

The allusion is clear, the gesture in a sense preordained. At least since Stuart Gilbert's 1957 edition of Joyce's letters, & subsequently reported in Ellmann's biography two years later, the story of Joyce's proposal to James Stephens to take over the work of completing *Finnegans Wake* has been widely repeated. The credulity, & just as earnest incredulity, with which Joyceans have greeted this piece of satire is probably a necessary symptom of a "Joyce Industry." The story goes that on 20 May 1927, Joyce, overwhelmed with the task at hand (somewhat prematurely as things turned out), proposed to Harriet Weaver that Stephens should be commissioned to wrap up his *Work-in-Progress*. He didn't get around to suggesting this directly to Stephens until two months later, when Stephens – who informed Joyce that *Anna Livia Plurabelle* was the "greatest prose ever written by a man" – promised to do everything he could to help, but that Joyce should finish the book himself, dah-dum.

Authorism & its Discontents

Joyce first met Stephens, who was a protégé of George Russell (Æ), in 1912 while he was struggling to publish *Dubliners* & while Stephens was in process of publishing his second novel, *The Crock of Gold* – a "mixture of philosophy, Irish folklore & the 'battle of the sexes,'" whose

---

[6] Iain Sinclair, *White Chappell, Scarlet Tracings* (London: Penguin, 2004 [1987]) 27.

[7] Iain Sinclair, *Downriver (Or, The Vessels of Wrath): A Narrative in Twelve Tales* (London: Grafton, 1991) 461.

[8] Sinclair, *Downriver*, 175.

"astringent use of irony," according to the *Encyclopaedia Britannica*, "suggests affinities with his friend James Joyce." In 1912, however, it is clear that neither Joyce nor Stephens considered the other a "friend" of any kind. As early as a letter to his brother Stanislaus in November 1909, Joyce had identified Stephens as a competitor, dubbing him "Ireland's latest genius" (*Letters* II, 260), & it was only after Joyce's ascendancy to the literary firmament, following the publication of *A Portrait* & *Ulysses*, that Joyce was able to indulge a condescending affinity for a rival on whom the tables had been turned.

Joyce's Oedipal/paternal relationship with Stephens belies all the niceties of Ellmann's line on "learning to become Joyce's contemporaries." It also exposes in Joyce's own "becoming contemporary" with Stephens (as with Shakespeare on a much more exulted plane) the singular precondition of killing the father in order to become the father – one of the overarching motifs of *Finnegans Wake*. And though Joyce never regarded Stephens as a "father" in any authorial way, the sense of his rival's having been anointed by the Dublin literary establishment ensured that, in *his* eyes, Stephens remained a proxy of precisely that paternal authority which, impervious to Joyce's importuning, would thereafter be compelled to recognize him.

It would be easy to regard Stephens as merely a footnote to the story of Joyce's wounded vanity, if it weren't for the fundamentally post-literary character of his assimilation into the Joycean narrative. According to this story, Joyce's proposal that Stephens – hereby elided with his own literary creation, *Stephen* Dedalus – should complete the *Wake*, where he himself was "unable" (a very sentimental inversion). This suggestion rested not on any writerly affinity, nor any shared purpose, but upon Joyce's superstition about a (mistakenly) shared birthday (if you wish to believe that) & the happy coincidence of their joint initials (in which they would "share" authorial credit) – JJ&S – being the branded acronym of John Jameson & Sons whiskey. Pure conceptualism, in other words.

In *Downriver*, Joblard – receiving Sinclair's similar proposition (or ultimatum), following a pilgrimage to the Isle of Sheppey – gets straight to the point:

> Is Sinclair completely gonzo? Has he screwed himself so deeply into his paranoid fantasies that he's imploded in a shatter of mutating icons. Does he *mean* it?
>
> I don't, of course, have to accept his spiked commission. Why should I strap myself to this improbable fictional double? Sinclair has exploited

– exclusively – the burlesque aspects of the role I have performed to gain acceptance in the world; & now he wants me to collude in this cheap trickery (this dreary post-modernist fraud) by writing as if I truly were this person he has chosen to exploit. My first difficulty. Which I intend sharply to counter by writing my account of the Sheppey journey as if he were imagining me writing it. In other words, I will write *my version* of him writing as me.[9]

Sinclair's turn upon Joyce's "James Stephens" trope – his proxification of Joblard as Shaun to his Shem, Jekyll to his Hyde – exposes both the parasitic & parricidal character of Joyce's omnivorous "contemporaneity": the world made word, the demiurge surrounded by automata. Reviewing Ellmann's biography, another Stephen, Spender this time, made the following remarks, worthy of being quoted at length:

> For Joyce the drug that led him into a trance was the obsessive fascination of coincidence & verbal play: Stephens & he both had the same first name – James; Stephens' second name was the one Joyce had chosen as first name for Stephen Dedalus; they were both born in Dublin on Feb. 2, 1882. The identification led him so far that he was seized with the fantastic idea that, if he were badly ill, or to die, James Stevens, his absolute alter ego, could complete "Finnegans Wake."
>
> There is a photograph of Joyce in this book with Stephens & with another of his identities or self-projections, John Sullivan, the singer. Joyce himself was a tenor; Sullivan was Irish, an exile, persecuted. That was enough. Joyce projected on to Sullivan all the tortures of his own sense of persecution by Dubliners, publishers, censors & the English.
>
> Mr Ellman's book thoroughly bears out an observation T.S. Eliot once made to me – that Joyce was the most completely self-centred man he had ever known. Even Joyce, modestly comparing himself with Ibsen, calls himself the lesser "egoarch." But to say that genius, which can turn the observed material of a lifetime into a world of art, is egotistic is not the same thing as to make the same judgment on anyone else.

Here, then, is a type of predicament. It would cost us no effort, in light of all this, to read Sinclair's psychogeographic meanderings as the tracings that they are: of a "literary" landscape *interpreted*, as Ellmann solicitously puts it, in advance by nothing less than that Leviathan of modernity we are invited – like Blake's lamb – to lie down beside. If *Downriver* maps a fluid space, "like" Joyce's *Wake*, of "memory, full of people, places, ideas, things, all with an ambiguous reality status" – a "densely textured narrative," as Angela Carter wrote in the *London Review of Books*, of

---

[9] Sinclair, *Downriver*, 380.

"ominous coincidence"[10] – this space emerges, with Joblard's previous appearance in the 1987 novel, *White Chappell, Scarlet Tracings*, from a type of cultural detritus, a *post-Wakean* converted mortuary for grubbers of first editions, museum fetishes.

Ellmann's historical contemporaneity has here been traded for a Joycean "no future," a set of bleak scenarios of repetition & re-enactment, framed by an anagram made out of the names of Jack-the-Ripper's victims: "Manac Es Cem, JK." An anagram, moreover, that recurs in the Lucia Anna Joyce section of Alan Moore's 2016 novel, *Jerusalem*, in a song verse "mad Lucia" is made to sing:

> Dusty's cunningly linguistic,
> Jem's misogynistic,
> But they dance the night away,
> Manac es cem, JK,
> And no more how's-your-father-now.
> Grinding signal into noise
> The crowd enjoys
> The final white parade.[11]

The proposition is death by inanition. In *Downriver*, Joblard appears disguised like Stephens & all of Hayman's Joycean epigones, to perpetuate, even in bad faith & with evident Schadenfreude, the great work & thereby "write *my version* of him writing as me."[12] Yet in *White Chappell* Joblard instead represents the other kind of Joycean avatar, appearing as if out of the very fabric of the narrative, "changeling, his face unset," though "full-grown, with no luggage, & a paleolithic past,"[13] as uncannily present as an agent holding a Mephisthophelean contract; at one moment pipe-smoking, the next bench-pressing, as if to say *everything has been calculated in advance*. He is the familiar forever threatening to collect, this Joblard figure, this Shemblable, always merging into an "identikit portrait"[14] in which – in the interminable "wake" of Joyce, whose "contemporaries" or "assassins" we are forever doomed to become or fail to become – the terminal "connection" is made, "the circuit completed."[15]

---

[10] Angela Carter, "Adventures at the End of Time," *London Review of Books* 13.5 (March, 1991): 17-18. She compares Downriver to Burroughs' *Naked Lunch*, quoting Kerouac: "an endless novel that would drive everybody mad." Again the unacknowledged allusion to Joyce.

[11] Alan Moore, *Jerusalem* (London: Knockabout, 2016) 871.

[12] Sinclair, *Downriver*, 40.

[13] Sinclair, *White Chappell, Scarlet Tracings*, 41.

[14] Sinclair, *White Chappell, Scarlet Tracings*, 87.

[15] Sinclair, *White Chappell, Scarlet Tracings*, 192.

Schizo-Cyberites

In the left-hand margin of "Cogito & the History of Madness," Derrida's 1963 essay on Foucault, an epigraph appears beneath a short quotation from Kierkegaard. It reads: "In any event this book was terribly daring. A transparent sheet separates it from madness. (Joyce, speaking of *Ulysses*)."[16] It's a description, as has often been noted, probably more befitting the work that came after *Ulysses*, or rather in its wake – separated by a "transparent sheet" of seventeen years during which time, as is by now well-known, Joyce's daughter descended progressively into that madness from which his writing so daringly maintained a prophylactic separation. Between 1922 & 1939, Lucia Anna Joyce was subjected to an array of unusual psychiatric treatments. These include – famously – botched therapy sessions with Jung & sea-water injections administered by the quack Henri Vignes, before she was briefly interned at St Andrews Hospital in Northampton, to which she returned after the War, dying there in 1982: "saltsick," into the arms of her "cold mad feary father."[17] She'd famously informed Nino Frank that the author of *Finnegans Wake* was indeed under the earth "watching us all the time."[18]

In his 2006 retracing of John Clare's "Journey out of Essex," *Edge of Orison*, Sinclair meditates – in one of several extended passages – on a 1923 sketch of Lucia by Myron Nutting: "Weight of hair, tilted head, eyes closed in concentration, pen in hand: the duty of composition. Winning paternal approval. Task set, with good intentions, by a troubled father: be what you are, my daughter. Demonstrate the gifts I gave you."[19] Depicted at work on her "lettrines," Lucia presents a picture of incapacity, "eyes closed," erased in the spectacle of becoming an iteration of the Joycean text she is literally tasked with ornamenting. (As, too, her biography would later, inevitably, become.) In Sinclair's rendering, she represents precisely an occasion: the occasion, anticipated in *Ulysses* & brought to fruition in the *Wake*, of a reification of a certain "night language"; an index of the unpresentable that, redeemed for a literary symptomatology, will instate a "reason of unreason," so to speak, "on the very borders

---

[16] Jacques Derrida, "Cogito & the History of Madness," *Writing & Difference*, trans. Alan Bass (London: Routledge, 1978) 31.

[17] Joyce, *Finnegans Wake*, 628.01.

[18] Ellmann, *James Joyce*, 743; from an interview with Nino Frank (1953).

[19] Iain Sinclair, *Edge of Orison: In the Traces of John Clare's "Journey out of Essex"* (London: Penguin, 2006) 69.

between being & non-being, between what is & what is not"[20] – or as Foucault says, between a history of reason & History *as* reason.

Sinclair's encounter with the figure of Lucia isn't entirely fortuitous. The coincidence, by way of place, with John Clare's confinement & loss of language – "word by word, syllable by syllable, letter by letter"[21] – extends, through another encounter, this time with Alan Moore, into a larger atavistic schema. Moore, who in *Edge of Orison* plays the Joblard role accompanying Sinclair to Lucia's grave, is quoted in the musings that follow as advancing "a relativist's General Theory of Northampton, loosely based on some late pronouncements by Stephen Hawking."[22] Published ten years later in the form of the twelve-hundred page "novel," *Jerusalem*, Moore's "General Theory" hinges around several key passages channelling Joyce's daughter – including a chapter entitled "Around the Bend" composed in cod-Wakese (it begins: "Awake, Lucia gets up…"[23] Her first appearance, however, comes almost a hundred pages earlier, "dancing on the madhouse lawn… Her Da, while living, sees her as a work in progress… but then he dies & leaves her stranded there in the excluded information, the ellipses…" Her family, Moore writes, "have edited her out, reduced her to a footnote in the yarn, all but excising her from the manuscript."[24]

Sinclair notes that, towards the end of her life, Lucia characterised herself with the words: "I mangle language,"[25] while in *Jerusalem* she becomes a figure of *Wakean* logorrhoea, both enunciator & enunciated, as if embodying a general textual relativity of a kind of *postliteraria biographia*. An Oulipian matrix. A conceptualist index. A "puzzle," as Moore says, endlessly productive of solutions, but which evades all effort at reduction. Jung diagnosed Lucia as Joyce's *anima inspiratrix*: the madness from which his "dreambook" separates itself by a transparent sheet & of which she is both the mimēsis & the de-generative operation. Joyce himself encoded her into the *Wake* as the very ontology of the text, evoking the genitive function of the *copula* in "Issy"; doubled as "Isis"; anagrammatically entangled, like recombinant DNA, in Joyce's own authorial proxy, HCE, as *Isolde* "the belle of Chapelizod": "her

---

[20] Alan Roughley, *Reading Derrida Reading Joyce* (Gainesville: University Press of Florida, 1999) 12.
[21] Sinclair, *Edge of Orison*, 239.
[22] Sinclair, *Edge of Orison*, 348.
[23] Moore, *Jerusalem*, 829.
[24] Moore, *Jerusalem*, 768.
[25] Sinclair, *Edge of Orison*, 348.

chaplet gardens," etc.[26] "Perhaps one day," Moore writes, Joyce would "have another go at her, fiddle with her a bit & try to sort out the stalled plotlines, all the uncompleted sentences..."[27]

The *Wake* adverts universally to such linguistic genomes, by means of which the kitsch of family romance is enlarged to cosmic proportions: a melodrama of archetypes – HCE & ALP, & their perpetual metonyms, Shem, Shaun & Issy. The latter triangle – evolving into complex manifolds of genetic disorder – rehearses all the failed (because incestuous) mutations of a text bound, as if in advance of itself, in the transparent membrane of its own negated future. In *Finnegans Wake*, Joyce evokes the nightmare of a self-contained totality, which in order to create itself must first discover a way out of itself, like a Pascalian avant-textual God Machine computing the odds of its own evolutionary possibility – by self-supersession, suicide, extinction-event, what-have-you. Such are the drolleries of every preliterate creation myth: to invent a future, the One aborts itself into Babelian "multiplicity" (History as metamatic *writing machine*). Yet such abortions are only ever a mimēsis of a prior, disavowed, difference at the origin: a primordial division, a schizo/phrenia already vested in the separation of the Book from madness.

Issy / Anna Livia / Lucia – a motif both of irreducible separation & impossible equivalence – describes (figuratively, at least) every abortion "along the winding ways of random ever"[28] of the copulative function of the verb *to be*, like a work-in-progress of mangled language. Enmeshed in sibling dysfunction with the Book's textual machinery – Shem the Pen, Shaun the Post – & lost in the reflection-effect of their double-negative "pseudoshamiana," she becomes the missing letter ("speech without words"[29]) in Joyce's post-literate language-mangle.[30] Mangled by language, "used out in sinscript,"[31] she comes to stand for all the expired mutations of sense out of which Joyce's holographic experiment proceeds. Like a coiled extra dimension, she is the consummate instant at which the

---

[26] Joyce, *Finnegans Wake*, 236.20; 265.14.
[27] Moore, *Jerusalem*, 768.
[28] Joyce, *Finnegans Wake*, 405.09.
[29] Joyce, *Finnegans Wake*, 174.10.
[30] On this point, Danis Rose makes the salient observation that it was only in 1933, on the cusp of Lucia being diagnosed with schizophrenia by Jung, that Joyce revised Issy's role in *Finnegans Wake* so as to give her a full "speaking part" in the sibling triangle mapped out in the "Nightlessons" episode. Danis Rose, *The Textual Diaries of James Joyce* (Dublin: Lilliput Press, 1995) 117.
[31] Joyce, *Finnegans Wake*, 421.18.

impossible is extruded into possibility & vice versa. If Shem is "mad" & Shaun "schisthematic rabblemint,"[32] Issy / Lucia nonetheless remains the rationale for Joyce's frantic purchase upon a post-literary futurity.

Danis Rose has gone so far as to assert an explicit connection between Joyce's struggle throughout the 1930s against the lack of "creative bursts" & the "free flow" of ideas that had characterized his earlier work on the *Wake*, with his "implacable resolve… never to accept defeat in the case of his daughter Lucia's decent into madness."[33] Though it begs the question: why not the contrary, also? There is the sense that, by accomplishing its "circular" closure, Joyce's book is able to trick the conjugative processes of causality (of "consecants & contangincies"[34]) into a general linguistic relativity, from which other "parallel" universes could emerge. It winds History back upon itself in a post-anterior movement of signifying-substitution, whose *spira mirabilis* would resolve into a *"Twofold Truth"* [35] that only *appears* – through Joyce's transparent sheet of language – to be "madness." His. Literature's.

Language without Words

But what would it mean, as Derrida says, "to write the history of this division"[36] – even if only to attempt its contrary? To write: a *history of*. Firstly, there is the question concerning mimēsis: of that ideally transparent sheet *of language* through which *ideas* communicate themselves to a signifying consciousness – between one consciousness & another – & so on. A seemingly invisible medium that nevertheless interferes in the flow of an ideal telepathy: language without words. As if to stand in the undisguised presence of God (Eidos), which would be madness. Reason, then, as separation from "pure reason." Or put it another way: writing as the mimēsis of a certain "madness"; "madness" as a *mimēsis of writing*. Of the crisis of History. Of a generalised Hysteria. *Des histoires*, etc.

This would seem to be the kernel of what presents itself to us in the *form* of *Finnegans Wake*: a writing destined to an impossible future, that can only ever be encountered as an open series of hyperstitional dead ends. It propagates by relentless dysfunction, a post-history of trial-by-

---

[32] Joyce, *Finnegans Wake*, 193.27; 424.36.
[33] Rose, *The Textual Diaries of James Joyce*, 115.
[34] Joyce, *Finnegans Wake*, 298.24.
[35] Joyce, *Finnegans Wake*, 305.L1.
[36] Derrida, "Cogito & the History of Madness," 43.

error: the "[o]bstinate murmur of a language that speaks by itself," as Foucault says, "without speaker or interlocutor, piled up upon itself, strangulated, collapsing before reaching the stage of formulation, quietly returning to the silence from which it never departed. The calcinated root of meaning."[37]

It is as if Joyce had sought to evoke the very contrary of *Ulysses*, his "terribly daring book" which, however much it gazed upon madness's work from behind the safety of that transparent sheet, remained *art*. In other words, a mimēsis conscious of itself as such. André Breton dismissed Joyce's 1922 book in precisely such terms:

> In opposition to the illusory stream of conscious associations, [Joyce] will present a flux & try to make it gush forth from all directions, a flux that in the last analysis tends to be the closest possible *imitation* of life (by means of which he keeps himself within the framework of *art*, falls once again into *novelistic* illusion, & fails to avoid being placed in the long line of naturalists & expressionists).[38]

It's for this reason that the *Wake* will not seek to imitate what lies beyond the transparent sheet separating it from whatever Joyce calls madness, but (as Beckett would have it[39]) to constitute that sheet itself: no longer "under the rubric of the capture or objectification,"[40] but of a certain presentiment. For again it is as if, through this window onto the Letheworld of the unconscious of language – of the unconscious *as* language – that Joyce intimates that crisis of reason that is writing's doppelganger. Since a writing that exceeds reason could not be contained within the metaphysical closure of a mimēsis, unless such a mimēsis were already the mark of the unpresentable itself, then the *Wake*'s "dissension" indeed marks "a self-dividing action, a cleavage & torment," as Derrida says, "interior to meaning in general."[41] And if the revolution of the word is thereby equated to a "revolution against reason," it isn't by means of a contrary depiction, lifting the "lifewand" so that the "dumb" may

---

[37] Qtd in Derrida, "Cogito & the History of Madness," 34-5.

[38] André Breton, "On Surrealism in its Living Works" [1953], trans. Richard Seaver & Helen R. Lane, in *Manifestoes of Surrealism* (Ann Arbor: University of Michigan Press, 1969) 298.

[39] "His [Joyce's] writing is not *about* something; *it is that something itself* [...] when the sense is sleep, the words go to sleep [...] when the sense is dancing, the words dance." Samuel Beckett, "Dante... Bruno, Vico.. Joyce," *Our Exagmination Round His Factification for Incamination of Work in Progress* (New York: New Directions Press, 1962) 14.

[40] Derrida, "Cogito & the History of Madness," 35.

[41] Derrida, "Cogito & the History of Madness," 36.

"speak,"[42] nor of a libratory "schizoanalysis" *à la* Guattari & Deleuze. Rather it is a question of what Joyce alludes to as *ambiviolence*.[43]

Simultaneously perturbative &, in a seemingly paradoxical movement, constitutive of a "system of sense," the radical ambivalence constituted in & by the *Wake* cannot simply be reduced to the kind of Hegelianism of a "revolution against reason" that "can be made only within it,"[44] since – evoking the figure of Babel (God's mangle). It is, as Derrida says, neither "construction nor ruin, but lability."[45] Its violence is no longer purely aesthetic but that of a generative poiēsis, capable of "soliciting" structure while also soliciting a countervailing *systemic* violence. Stated otherwise: it produces the system of its own interpretation & of the interpretative violence by which it would be reduced, as Kierkegaard says, to the "madness" of decision, of *univocity*.[46] It represents a "revolution against reason" in the form, precisely, of its own unpresentability, since in order to signify first the text itself must disappear or "decenter" itself, withdrawing from the field of semantic potential it appears simultaneously to summon forth. As Guattari argues, apropos of the linguistic/machinic unconscious, "There is no meta-language here. The collective assemblage of enunciation speaks 'on the same level' as states of affairs, states of facts, & subjective states."[47]

It is from such circumstances that *différance*, in the Derridean lexicon, draws its force, as neither word nor concept[48] – that is to say, as being irreducible to a mimēsis. The *Wake*'s "ambiviolence" thus encodes within itself the deformations of that transparent separation upon which the language of reason – of signs-to-concepts, of mimēsis – hinges. It is, in

---

[42] Joyce, *Finnegans Wake*, 195.5-6.

[43] See Stephen Heath, "Ambiviolences: Notes for reading Joyce," trans. Isabelle Mahieu, in *Poststructuralist Joyce: Essays from the French*, eds. Derek Attridge & Daniel Ferrer (Cambridge: Cambridge University Press, 1984) 46.

[44] "There is no Trojan horse unconquerable by Reason (in general). The unsurpassable, unique & imperial grandeur of the order of reason... is that one cannot speak out against it except by being for it, that one can only protest against it from within it." Derrida, "Cogito & the History of Madness," 36.

[45] Jacques Derrida, "Force & Signification," *Writing & Difference*, trans. Alan Bass (London: Routledge, 1978) 6.

[46] "The Instant of Decision is Madness (Kierkegaard)," qtd in Derrida, "Cogito & the History of Madness," 31.

[47] Félix Guattari, *The Machinic Unconscious*, trans. Taylor Adkins (Los Angeles: Semiotext(e), 2011), 14.

[48] Jacques Derrida, "Différance," *Margins of Philosophy*, trans. Alan Bass (Chicago: Chicago University Press, 1982) 4-5.

its "objective correlative," a subversion of subversion that, "like" the figure of Lucia, begets in a certain *writing after* the *Wake* a negative genealogy. Sinclair's "hypnotized sleepwalker's dance," for example, "movements choreographed by alienists"[49] (alluding to a photo Beckett retained as a keepsake of that abortive liaison between himself & Joyce's daughter, "occurring," as Moore astutely observed, "in an atmosphere of incest"[50]). For if Lucia herself is the kernel of a certain madness incipient in *Finnegans Wake*, "she" is also the matrix of its propagation, so to speak, of a genealogical antagonism of post-literature, from Joyce to Beckett, to Sinclair, to Moore & beyond: "honor[ing] commercio's energy yet aid[ing] the linkless proud, the plurable with everybody & ech with pal."[51]

If Lucia is made to stand for some kind of epigenetic *id* to the Joycean *ego*, it is nonetheless an *id* remote from those avatars of Romantic agonism & the trope of the "mad woman in the attic" – she represents, *insofar as she represents anything*, "neither the primordial nor the instinctual"; & if her embodiments of language is described as "*elemental*" they are, as Lacan says, "no more [so] than the *elements of the signifier*."[52] As Deleuze writes, "Languages are gibberish, Joycean quirks; they are not anchored in structures. It is only functions & movements that manage to create a bit of polemical order in them."[53] From Joyce's incest machine, everything that emerges is, in a sense, simply one more anagrammatically mangled morphogenesis on its way to becoming structure (Anna's grammar); one more roll of dice, as Mallarmé says, in the deterministic circuit of resurrected chance; one more *post*. It is as if, speaking from a secret reservoir of meaning, this cybernetics of an incessant incest-after-the-fact presents the anachronistic image of an archē & telos of linguistic sense to which "the book" & all its literary metonyms – separated from it by a seemingly transparent sheet, & despite everything – impossibly refer.

It's for this reason that *Finnegans Wake* may be said to accomplish itself as the unique specimen of its genre. Its radical compulsion to repeat corresponds to an equally radical singularity: a genealogical unicum, wherein all that comes in its wake is the post-productive "sterility" of self-

---

[49] Sinclair, *Edge of Orison*, 238.

[50] Moore, *Jerusalem*, 768.

[51] Joyce, *Finnegans Wake*, 264.1-3. Where *ech* = HCE & *pal* = ALP, which combined produce CHAPEL (i.e. Chapel-Isolde, etc.).

[52] Jacques Lacan, "The Insistence of the Letter in the Unconscious," *Écrits*, trans. Bruce Fink (New York: Norton, 2006) 434.

[53] Gilles Deleuze, "The Future of Linguistics," *Two Regimes of Madness: Texts & Interviews 1975-1995*, trans. A. Hodge & M. Taormina (New York: Semiotext(e), 2006) 71.

interpolation (Moore's unintentionally parodic Wakese, Sinclair's stock-in-trade syntactical "effects," etc. – up to & including Lucia's mangled language). Within the circuit of its recurrence, Joyce's Babelian textual machine perpetually closes the circle in order to generate an opening for an illicit *surplus-jouissance*: the fantasized unity of an impossible incest; the self-signifying totality of the Word.

CONSPIRACIES OF NO FUTURE

> Man is the ideology of dehumanisation.
> — Theodor Adorno, *The Jargon of Authenticity*

The "neutrality" dogma of technical systems in the evolution of the posthuman idea is one that paradoxically situates humanity as a (future) being unveiled in time. This dogma simultaneously transcends mere "temporality" by virtue of an access to historical consciousness or what Heidegger termed the "locus" of its system.[1] At least since Hegel, it devolved upon a twofold understanding:

1. "the abstraction of *consuming*" (Abstraktion des Verzehrens), i.e., the temporal mode of becoming as a "transition from being to nothing or from nothing to being" exemplified in the productivism of Hegel's "negation of a negation"[2]; or

2. "'*intuited*' becoming," i.e., *circulation* (Marx) or "the transition which does not get thought but which simply tenders itself in the sequence of 'nows.'"[3]

This temporality of becoming is a constant presence that is "monstrously privileged" in the Hegelian system.[4] Time "itself" is the dimension of the unthought *par excellence*, defining a primordial situation into which the idea of humanity is introduced as a mechanism of dialectical unveiling. Stemming from its inexplicable character, the introduction of the human hypothesis exacerbates its appearance of artificiality. The revelation of humanity *being* "mediated" in advance by an externalised agency (e.g., historical consciousness & the idea that history is mnemotechnic) is complemented by the contingency that "man" has disclosed points to the concomitant necessity of accounting for the status of the human. This status entails an abstract *interval* that causes (or allows) the temporal *to be thought* – firstly as an "indifferent subsistence" of difference (Heidegger), & secondly as technē.

Such an "intervention" in the primordiality of time & its reification in the "abstraction of consuming" suggests a trajectory of humanism.

---

[1] Martin Heidegger, *Being & Time*, trans. J. Macquarie & E. Robinson (London: Blackwell, 1992 [1926]) 429. All page references are, according to convention, to the German edition cited in the margins of the English translation.

[2] Heidegger, *Being & Time*, 431; 432.

[3] G.W.F. Hegel, *Encyclopaedia*, §258, *addendum*; cited in Heidegger, *Being & Time*, 431.

[4] In contrast, Heidegger indicates an anachronistic core of the being of time: "The primary phenomenon of primordiality & authentic temporality is the future" (*Being & Time*, 378).

This happens through various stages of socio-technological change & appears to culminate – via a latter-day expression of Herbert Spencer's evolutionary philosophy of the "inevitability of progress"[5] – in the advent of the global commodity system & mass-medialised consumer culture. What used to be called the "Ends of Man" with a certain naïve optimism, & what has come to be subsumed in the conflation of an "End of History" with the "Sixth Extinction Event," is located in the disclosure of a *radical technicity* at the core of humanism. (Heideggerianism, despite itself, revolves around a conception of Dasein as the *subjectivity of technē*).

Terminal Humanism

In a passage as often misunderstood as it is quoted, Heidegger says technology is a "challenge posed to humanity."[6] This challenge is also a *confrontation*. It emerges from a crisis in the doctrinal certainties of humanism & the ideology of "the human" as *animal rationale*, alongside a critique of time-consciousness, & the appeal to a pure philosophy of "history" untrammelled by the experience of technicity. In Heidegger's quest to "open our human existence to the essence of technology,"[7] the relationship between the disclosure of being as phenomenality & the disclosure of being as discursivity (i.e., the "technē of inscription") comes to be increasingly at issue. In its technological sense, disclosure – as complementarily phenomenal & discursive – acquires what Maurice Merleau-Ponty has referred to as a "motor significance" that, in turn, defines a "motor physiognomy" comprised of "motor reactions," each of which signals the amplification of our "motor being."[8]

In the relation of the semantic evolution of "man" to a certain technology of "motility" (Merleau-Ponty calls it "basic intentionality"[9]), human existence acquires the tenor of a "motor subject" whose being accedes to a materiality of discourse by way of an event (Ereignis). The event constitutes an accession to a certain ontico-temporal prosthesis that is symbolised, at least since the Industrial Revolution, in humanity's relationship to the machine. This generalisation belongs to the worldly

---

[5] Herbert Spencer, *Principles of Sociology*, 2 vols. (New York: D. Appleton, 1897 [1876-96]).
[6] Martin Heidegger, "The Question Concerning Technology," *Basic Writings*, ed. David Farrell Krell (London: Routledge, 1993) 311.
[7] Heidegger, "The Question Concerning Technology," 311.
[8] Maurice Merleau-Ponty, *Phenomenology of Perception*, trans. Colin Smith (London: Routledge & Kegan Paul, 1962) 211.
[9] Merleau-Ponty, *Phenomenology of Perception*, 158-9.

inasmuch as it belongs to a being-in-the-world. It describes a virtuality or event-state in the constitution of the technological situation of the human.

Such a non-instrumental, technologically disclosed conception of the human accords with the logic of what Derrida elsewhere terms a "prosthesis at the origin" (i.e., the "originary intrusion, the ageless intrusion of technics"[10]), as if in place of (or in *anticipation* of) a formalised agency vested in either a Cartesian *cogito me cogitare rem* or a Hegelian *time & "spirit"* as the essence of a *conscientia*.[11] The primordial *state* of temporality into which the human is supposedly interpolated in the Hegelian schema is thereby revealed to be already opened to the possibility of such an "intervention," since the possibility of the human's disclosure is already the interval of this temporality. This is the case even if we only understand it as an instantiation of the "now" since it has been a matrix of *technological event-states* from its "origin."

Subsequently for Marx, the machine no longer represents a counter- or post-humanistic development. The machine is now the "essence" of humanism. The limitations of the definition of technology – a "means to an end" (instrumentum), or a human "activity," marking an intervention in an otherwise primordial state of affairs ("the differentiation at the heart of the social multiplicity: the division of labour"[12]) – are not so much overcome as transduced in an understanding of the "social evolution" of the human idea. This idea concerns the three-fold relation of nature (the given status of man), reason (the deduced status of man), & technology (the produced status of man). It is linked to a movement that is historical only insofar as the historical is always an after-effect of whatever it is that can be said to *inaugurate* humanism. Such an "evolutionary" movement always seems to occur independently of the human man & no longer represents a dialectical unveiling, as in Hegel & Marx. There is a "crisis" in the logic of historical thesis, primordiality, causal agency & the ego cogito. Once again, the crisis is signalled within the ongoing critique of modernity in the recursive trope of "the machine." ("The time of modernity," writes Nancy, "is followed by the time of things."[13])

What, then, is humanity's *true life*?

---

[10] Jacques Derrida, *On Touching – Jean-Luc Nancy*, trans. Christine Irizarry (Stanford : Stanford University Press, 2005) 113.

[11] Cf. Heidegger, *Being & Time*, 433.

[12] Gilles Deleuze, *Difference & Repetition*, trans. Paul Patton (London: Continuum, 2001 [1968]) 207.

[13] Jean-Luc Nancy, "Changing of the World," trans. Steven Miller, *A Finite Thinking*, ed. Simon Sparks (Stanford: Stanford University Press, 2003) 318.

Lewis Mumford recounts that utilitarianism has always had a ready answer because "it consisted in having more wants than could be supplied by the machine, & inventing more ways in which these wants could be varied & expanded."[14] But industrial man has never simply been a function of productive stimulus & aesthetic response vis-à-vis a mechanical world that stands in place of & simulates the real, natural world of experience & desire. The human has never been some sort of autonomous zone of variability or expandable wants in relation to the satisfaction of these wants, other than in the sense that want itself (or even desire) supposes something like a prosthesis, a supplement, an extension of what is necessarily or essentially human. This is the ideological basis of humanism in its most general sense. The challenge posed by technology is thus not a challenge to humanity as such, but a challenge posed to certain ideological discourses of "man" that, lacking any sustainable claim upon a more foundational metaphysics, have in recent times entered into a series of "crises." Consider the kind evoked by Ernst Cassirer in *Essay on Man* (1944): "Man's claim to being the centre of the universe has lost its foundation. Man is placed in an infinite space in which his being seems to be a single & vanishing point. He is surrounded by a mute universe, by a world that is silent to his religious feeling & his deepest moral demands."[15]

Consequently, it is the *idea* of humanity (& its domination by a certain *eugenicist* logic) that has most come to be placed in question & "alienated" by the evolution or socalled progress of modern technology. "In no other period of human knowledge," argues Max Scheler, "has man ever become so problematic to himself than in our own days. We have a scientific, a philosophical, & a theological anthropology that know nothing of each other. Therefore we no longer possess any clear & consistent idea of man. The ever-growing multiplicity of the particular sciences that are engaged in the study of men has much more confused & obscured than elucidated our concept of man."[16]

And yet, at least since the Renaissance, scientific discourse has entailed a materialist foundation that has increasingly tended to define this anthropocentric "world" in *probabilistic* terms. This has held true even while the "facts" comprising it have acquired a certain *universality* & *immanence* within the ideological formation of humanism. John Dewey writes:

---

[14] Lewis Mumford, *The Condition of Man* (London: Martin Secker & Warburg, 1944) 304.

[15] Ernst Cassirer, *An Essay on Man* (New Haven: Yale University Press, 1944) 13-4.

[16] Max Scheler, *Die Stellung des Menschen im Kosmos* (Darmstadt: Reichl, 1928) 13f; cited in Cassirer, *An Essay on Man*, 22.

> The universality that belongs to scientific theories is not that of inherent content fixed by God or Nature, but of a range of applicability – of capacity to take events out of their apparent isolation so as to order them into systems which (as is the case with all living things) prove they are alive by the kind of change which is *growth*. From the standpoint of scientific inquiry, nothing is more fatal to its right to obtain acceptance than a claim that its conclusions are final & hence incapable of a development that is other than mere quantitative extension.[17]

Within the implied essentialism of humanity's "factual world," pragmatics & idealism enter into an unacknowledged compact that threatens to obscure the prosthetic character of this world, which is empirically delineated as well as construed. The "facts of science," Cassirer asserts, "always imply a theoretical, which means a symbolic, element."[18] Furthermore, "it is symbolic thought which overcomes the natural inertia of man & endows him with a new ability, the ability to constantly reshape his human universe."[19] The possibility of this reshaping, expressed as the "discourse of man," situates technics, the "system of human activities," within a broader technological discourse that Jacques Lacan terms "the realm of the symbolic." This necessarily implies the realm of the machine (all machines, including the socalled organic, are symbolic machines).[20] What is more, this implication of the mechanical is a general condition of symbolisation that renders the "human condition" a metonymic counterpart.

For this reason, the "question concerning technology" requires that we look beyond the world of technical facts to the status of humanity as a *technological being*. In effect, we move towards an investigation into the meaning of technology as such. "Technology," Heidegger famously argues, "is not *equivalent* to the *essence* of technology […] Likewise, the essence of technology is by no means anything technological. Thus we shall never experience our relationship to the essence of technology so long as we merely represent & pursue the technological, put up with it, or evade it."[21] It is necessary, in other words, to account not only for the constitutive, but also conditional enlargement of the lifeworld of "man" beyond its assumed artefactual basis. By way of technological "progress,"

---

[17] John Dewey, *Reconstruction in Philosophy* (Boston: Beacon Press, 1957 [1920]) xv-xvi.

[18] Cassirer, *An Essay on Man*, 59.

[19] Cassirer, *An Essay on Man*, 62.

[20] Jacques Lacan, "A Materialist Definition of Consciousness," *The Seminar of Jacques Lacan. Book II: The Ego in Freud's Theory & in the Technique of Psychoanalysis 1954-1955*, trans. S. Tomaselli (London: Cambridge University Press, 1988) 47.

[21] Heidegger, "The Question Concerning Technology," 311 – emphasis added.

humanity has discovered a method for self-adaptation as much as a radical disclosure of our technological situation.

Ghosts of Futures Past

Since the Industrial Revolution, & particularly since the mid-nineteenth century, the human idea has increasingly converged on its own reification in the discourse of labour, the free market & commodification with regard to the advent of industrialisation, which comes to define a *universal*, abstract characteristic later associated with Dasein. Whether we look towards the early discourses of economic liberalism (Adam Smith) or industrial socialism (Robert Owen), we inevitably discover the figure of labour emerging to "complete" the dialectic of humanism by firstly introducing the machine in the place of a rational, mechanical (Newtonian) god, & secondly by putting it in the place of a rational (Cartesian) subject. This emergence is then concretised, as Mumford suggests, by a further two-fold movement:

1. the machine, by removing all "fixed, fast, frozen relations ... caused man to face ... the real conditions of his life";

2. in doing so, the machine became constitutive of man's consciousness of the "real conditions of his life," so that it is in fact "the technological developments that secure man's existence."[22]

The challenge posed to humanity is not simply a matter of designating "man" as a being-for the machine, but in the disclosure that the category of "man" is first & foremost technological. The risk is not that mankind will be supplanted by & enslaved to the machine. But humanity might finally learn to recognise itself in technology as the yet-to-be-thought *rationale* of the human hypothesis.

The transformation of humanist thought during the Industrial Revolution – & the failure of earlier humanistic accounts to sustain the idea of a human-centred universe – has often been portrayed as a movement of technological nihilism according to which the individual (& the individual's "freedom-of-the-will") is supplanted by a mechanical uniformity & "mass" consciousness. The spectre of nihilism, however, can more often than not be seen as a symptom of a "will to mastery" that "becomes all the more urgent the more technology threatens to slip from human control."[23] Even in its most autonomous or most

---

[22] Mumford, *The Condition of Man*, 330-1.
[23] Heidegger, "The Question Concerning Technology," 313.

inhuman manifestations, technology doesn't represent a cold-blooded withdrawal from life or from humanity. What we call inhumanity stands as a question of humanity's accountability to itself. Technology represents the disclosure of a properly human domain & an idea of the individual *commensurate with its time* (i.e., commensurate with what Heidegger calls the *time of being*).

Bernard Stiegler has proposed that the temporal relation between man & technology is a solicitation of a social order or social apparatus. No longer is this relation a collective metaphor of the historical unfolding of human destiny or destining. Now it is a σύστημα: a *system* or *technē* of human evolution.[24] The socius cannot be recognised in terms of an organisation reified into the (politico-mimetic) institutions of "law, state, church, family, friendship, industrial association,"[25] as Dewey says. It must be viewed as an emergent mode of discourse wherein the dichotomy of individual & society is transfigured into a dynamic relation of complementarity, recursivity, & reflexive temporality. (Similarly, in the history of science, self-criticism affected a "shaking up [...] which loosened the firm hold of earlier cosmology"[26]). However, recurrence & the counter-logic of the discrete event are never located in a single dimension or instant "in time," as it were, but in the technē of a temporalisation that is essentially distanciated or tele-technological. This allows for a certain duration in each of the spatial dimensions of what we call *transcription*. Being, in this sense, is "temporally inscribed" within the recursive, quasi-periodic structure of a technicity that is generalised in the discourse of humanism as its teleological stereotype.

Forecasted in the work of Marx, this discourse has come more starkly into view in the serial catastrophism of globalisation & the transformed constellation of the Anthropocene under the conditions of informatic deterritorialisation & the nano-metrics of hyper-commodification. Marx's early investigations into the commodity identified the processes of *alienation* inherent in the relation of individual-as-labour to

---

[24] Bernard Stiegler, *Technics & Time. Volume I: The Fault of Epimetheus*, trans. Richard Beardsworth & George Collins (Stanford: Stanford University Press, 1998).

[25] Dewey, *Reconstruction in Philosophy*, 188.

[26] Dewey, *Reconstruction in Philosophy*, xix. This "temporality" enlarges the experience of being by way of a technics of futurity, & hence of virtuality (what Heidegger terms a "standing reserve" or Bestand), whereby what is most timely is man's access to being in its symbolic, discursive dimension. That is to say, as a *forethrow* of signification – whereby "being" is distinguished from the conventional notion of "organic life" which exists only insofar as it evolves in socalled present time.

industrial modes of production (i.e., the consequence of a process of *technologisation*). Marx also identified the alienism of a particular idea of "man" who was no longer merely posed as the *adversary* of technical production. Moreover, the tenacity of this alienism necessarily increases the more the "representation of technology" comes to negate & supersede a primitive adversarialism (i.e., as its human stereotype).[27] Alienation, then, is commensurate with a realisation that the techno-humanist "condition" points towards the historical supersession of the individual-as-commodified-labour & of labour "time." Consequently, the prospect of a *post*-industrialisation – the "*indefinitely extensible* consumption of superfluities," Thorstein Weblen diagnosed[28] – becomes a threat to those discourses, which are exemplified in Weber's protestant work ethic,[29] & which define the human by way of a redemption-through-labour that conceals the god-in-man within will-to-productivity & later in will-to-consumption.

Debord makes a comparable point. He argues that the abstraction of labour time paradoxically affirms the concreteness of humanity's "individualised" status within the commodity spectacle. Stiegler observes that such labour is "the process of modification of the individual stereotype, repetitive anticipation of the stereotype being only the archē-form of this temporality."[30] Debord says: "The spectacle originates in the loss of the unity of the world, & the gigantic expansion of the modern spectacle expresses the totality of this loss: the abstraction of all specific labour & the general abstraction of the entirety of production are perfectly rendered in the spectacle, whose *mode of being concrete* is precisely abstraction." Consequently, the "worker does not produce himself; he produces an independent power. The *success* of this production, its abundance, returns to the producer as an *abundance of dispossession*. All the time & space of his world become *foreign* to him with the accumulation of his alienated products. The spectacle is the map of this new world, a map which exactly covers its territory."[31] Likewise, it is only in the transformation of

---

[27] Cf. Karl Marx, "Economic & Philosophical Manuscripts," *Early Writings*, intro. Lucio Colletti (London: Penguin, 1975), 324-5.

[28] Thorstein Weblen, *The Theory of the Leisure Class: An Economic Study of Institutions* (New York: New American Library, 1953 [1899]) 60ff.

[29] Max Weber, *The Protestant Ethic & the Spirit of Capitalism*, trans. Talcott Parsons (New York: Charles Scribner's Sons, 1958).

[30] Stiegler, *Technics & Time*, 159.

[31] Guy Debord, *The Society of the Spectacle*, trans. Donald Nicholson-Smith (New York: Zone Books, 1995) §29; §31. This then leads Debord to express the stereotypical status of the

manufacture via technicity (i.e., via the machine & of the commodity) that the "human-abstract" is transformed from an image of discrete production to one of socalled continuous consumption *as* spectral accumulation (vis-à-vis the media-technological turn of post-industrialisation). Technology, in this sense, eludes the rigid stratifications & rigidifications of ideology, & manifests the open possibility of a generalised, spectral "capitalisation." This occurs, above all, in the phenomenon of globalisation already anticipated by Marx in 1872.[32]

Of Alienation Born

Marx's preparatory study for *A Contribution to the Critique of Political Economy* (1859) & *Capital* (1867) was posthumously published as the *Grundrisse der Kritik der Politischen Ökonomie* in 1939-41. In it, he undertook an analysis of the relation of labour to technology as a function of temporalisation. He began with a critique of machinery as labour-saving (i.e., as productive of surplus labour & labour *time*)[33] & moved towards the thesis that labour is thereby transformed into a "living accessory" of the machine. In this latter sense, the machine ceases to be regarded in terms of socalled fixed capital & acquires a unique symbolic function in the translation of "necessary labour time" (which works for mere use-value or subsistence) into "surplus labour time" (which represents work for "exchange value").[34] This circulation of value is the "necessary surplus" of symbolic exchange. It is underwritten by the machine's capacity to produce the appearance of a standing reserve of labour time through "the reduction of the number of necessary workers" so that technicity extends from an extractive to a formative function in isolating & quantifying labour temporally. Additionally, technicity acts upon its discursive character (e.g., its potentiality).[35]

As a result of this discursive characteristic, the production of standing reserve acquires a signifying function by virtue of its investment in a certain "futurity" bound to the materiality of "time

---

human-abstract in terms of the well-known formula: "The spectacle is *capital* to such a degree of accumulation that it becomes an image" §34.

[32] Karl Marx & Friedrich Engels, *The Communist Manifesto*, trans. Samuel Moore, intro. A.J.P. Taylor (London: Penguin, 1967) 83ff.

[33] Karl Marx, *Outlines of the Critique of Political Economy*, trans. Martin Nicolaus (London: Penguin, 1973) 389.

[34] Marx, *Outlines of the Critique of Political Economy*, 767-8.

[35] See Deleuze, *Difference & Repetition*, 186.

in hand." Time, however, is not limited to a quantifiable "structure of occurrence." It constitutes what we might call an event-state where the "potentiality" of any standing reserve possesses a formal relation to technology & is a mechanism of "objectless occurrence" or generalised possibility. That is, time discloses a *signifying* function, "productive of meaning," rather than a function of rigid designation (or a type of *temporalised mimēsis*).

The significance of "the machine" for Marx extends beyond the production-transformation dichotomy defined by the mathematician Charles Babbage. In Marx's view, Babbage divides machines into two categories: "(1) machines employed to produce power; (2) machines whose purpose is simply to transmit power & to perform the work."[36] Later biologists & cyberneticists come to call this *autopoiēsis*: the capacity of a machine or mechanism to transform & reproduce itself.[37] The autopoetic dimension of technicity in Marx's conception devolves into a certain recursive ambivalence between inertia & dynamics (i.e., entropy) in the illusory structure of "fixed capital." According to Marx:

> Capital which consumes itself in the production process, or fixed capital, is the *means of production* in the strict sense. In a broader sense the entire production process & each of its movements, such as circulation – as regards its material side – is only a means of production for capital, for which value alone is the end in itself ... But the determination that the use value of fixed capital is that which eats itself up in the production process is identical to the proposition that it is used in this process only as a means, & itself exists merely as an *agency* for the transformation of the raw material into the product. As such a means of production, its use value can be that it is merely the technological condition for the occurrence of the process (the site where the production process proceeds) ... or that it is the direct condition of the action of the means of production proper, like all *matières instrumentales*. Both are in turn only the material presuppositions for the production process generally.[38]

Consequently, the autoconsumptive, autopoetic relation of agency to the production of value must be rethought in terms of a material condition or, as Marx says, a presupposition that has a "potentiated" dynamic ambivalence.[39] This ambivalence solicits the processual system that otherwise considers it to be a mere adjunct, characteristic, or solicitation

---

[36] Cited in Marx, *Outlines of the Critique of Political Economy*, 690.
[37] See Humberto Maturana & Francisco Varela, *Autopoiesis & Cognition* (Boston: Reidal, 1979).
[38] Marx, *Outlines of the Critique of Political Economy*, 690-1.
[39] Cf. Deleuze, *Difference & Repetition*, 91.

of value *qua* value (i.e., a gradient of probabilities across which the production of standing-reserve is distributed in a relation to future possible modes of exchange). In this scenario, the human – a locus of future exchange (i.e., of what is to be disclosed) – approximates a tropic figure. Agency affects this figure "automatically" in a series of processual event-states whose material condition is "exchangeability."

Humanity is thereby not simply "what it makes of itself,"[40] as Sartre insists. Humanity *is constituted* by virtue of a condition that simultaneously closes it off from the prior assumption of an inaugurating selfhood & makes it into a *prosthesis* of technological agency. According to Marx, "labour appears [...] merely as a *conscious organ*" distributed among the "numerous points of the mechanical system, subsumed under the total process of the machinery itself."[41] Hence technology (an End of History) supplants the Ends of Man as the "truth" or "essence" of metaphysical thought so that, like Sartre's pronouncements vis-à-vis ontology, the concept of *humanitas* "has merely enabled us to determine the ultimate ends of human reality, its fundamental possibilities, & the value which haunts it."[42]

This total process moves from the "psychotechnics" of Taylorism & Fordism to the techno-mediality of McLuhan's communicating systems.[43] It puts humanity in a twofold relation to the determination of being: on the one hand, its (indeterminate) horizon of possibility; on the other hand, its necessary & recursive decidability. In both cases, the figure of humanity stands in relation to a total process within & against which its status is supersession. It is, as Derrida & Stiegler both argue, impossible for humanity to *choose* technology, as though technology existed in an objective relation to an already complete idea of the human.[44] Humanity (e.g., via the trope of labour) is the fictional locus of a *choosing*, of an interminable & impossible decision. This does not represent a formal transposition of the idea of the human from, say, a Cartesian to a Marxian register. It represents

---

[40] Jean-Paul Sartre, "The Humanism of Existentialism," *Essays in Existentialism*, ed. Wade Baskin (Secaucus, N.J.: Citadel Press, 1965) 36.

[41] Marx, *Outlines of the Critique of Political Economy*, 694.

[42] From *Being & Nothingness*, cited as one of three epigraphs to Derrida's 1968 lecture, "The Ends of Man," *Margins of Philosophy*, trans. Alan Bass (Chicago: Chicago University Press, 1982) 111.

[43] Cf. Anson Rabinach, *The Human Motor: Energy, Fatigue, & the Origins of Modernity* (Berkeley: University of California Press, 1992) 278.

[44] Jacques Derrida & Bernard Stiegler, "The Archive Market: Truth, Testimony, Evidence," *Echographies of Television*, trans. Jennifer Bayorek (Cambridge: Polity, 2002) 46.

a fundamental shift in the conception of humanity (via the figure of the *individual*) as a *prosthesis of reason*. As Marx's analysis of the labour relation makes clear, the status of *consciousness* requires it to be re-thought in terms of an "automaton" of agency vested in a *signifying materiality*:

> As long as the means of labour remains a means of labour in the proper sense of the term, such as it is directly, historically, adopted by capital & included in its realisation process, it undergoes a merely formal modification, by appearing now as a means of labour not only in regard to its material side, but also at the same time as a mode of the presence of capital, determined by its total process – as *fixed capital*. But, once adopted into the production process of capital, the means of labour passes through different metamorphoses, whose culmination is the *machine*, or rather, an *automated system of machinery*... set in motion by an automaton, a moving power that moves itself; this automaton consisting of numerous mechanical & intellectual organs, so that the workers themselves are cast merely as its conscious linkages.[45]

Marx identifies the machinic in Heideggerian terms. For him, the machinic is a mode of revealing an "essential [technological] being" of which (by a Freudian counterpoint) "fixed capital" is the *fundamental fantasy*. The turn in Marx's early thinking – from quantitative equivalence between the productive force of labour & "the productive forces of industry & technology"[46] to a recognition of labour power[47] that forms a paradigm for recursive production & circulation of value – posits the mechanisation of humanity's own-most capacity for being-in-the-world *as alienation*.

Humanity's "freedom" cannot be purchased *by way of* technology or at the price of the replacement of the "individual" by the machine. At risk of involving a metaphysical reduction, our "freedom" must be(get) a confrontation within the technological "essence" of the condition for individuated being (i.e. "its conscious linkages"). This is not a purely tropic movement (e.g., from metaphorical equivalence to metonymic recursion) wherein "freedom" becomes an operation across or between such contiguities. Nor is it limited to the insistence that technology "is merely abstract labour operating with 'indifference.'"[48] Rather, it is a

---

[45] Marx, *Outlines of the Critique of Political Economy*, 692-3.
[46] Along with the conception of labour as "the quintessentially human activity defining social being & offering humanity the way to re-appropriate & regain its essential attributes." Rabinach, *The Human Motor*, 72-3.
[47] Arbeitskraft, i.e. "increased productivity & greater intensity of labour" as functions of labour time. Karl Marx, *Capital: A Critique of Political Economy*, vol. 3 (London: Penguin, 1976) 666-7.
[48] Rabinach, *The Human Motor*, 78.

movement tied to the immanence of supersession, which is a mechanism of disclosure. The individual obtains this movement in the form of the recursive, co-ordinate term *par excellence*, operating upon the minimal differentiality of inchoate value. Technology, "freed" of its prosthetic relation to the idea of the human, gives birth to humanity as the anticipated "end-in-itself" of technopoetic agency. Hence the following:

> In no way does the machine appear as the individual worker's means of labour. Its distinguishing characteristic is not in the least, as with the means of labour, to transmit the worker's activity to the object; this *activity*, rather, is posited in such a way that it merely transmits the machine's work, the machine's action, on to the raw material – supervises it & guards against interruptions. Not as with the instrument, which the worker animates & makes into his organ with his skill & strength, & whose handling therefore depends on his virtuosity. Rather, it is the machine which possesses skill & strength in place of the worker, is itself the virtuoso, with a soul of its own in the mechanical laws *acting through it*… The worker's activity, reduced to a mere *abstraction of activity*, is determined & regulated on all sides by the movement of the machinery, & not the opposite.[49]

In this way, Marx echoes Pascal's ruminations from two centuries earlier on the machine & the optimisation of input-output performance. According to Pascal, the measure of a machine's performance entails its speed & accuracy as much as its capacity to both expropriate & render dispensable "a certain number of mental operations" deemed necessary for a "human calculator." For this reason, "the most ignorant person finds in [the machine] as great an advantage as the most experienced; the instrument supplies the defect of ignorance or lack of habit &, by necessary movements, it performs all alone, without even the intention of the user, all the abridgements possible to nature."[50] The machine is the ideal prosthesis of accelerated, surplus-production expenditure of labour. Likewise, Marx observes: "The science which compels the inanimate limbs of the machinery, by their construction, to act purposefully, as an automaton, does not exist in the worker's consciousness, but rather acts upon him through the machine as an alien power, as the power of the machine itself."[51]

---

[49] Marx, *Outlines of the Critique of Political Economy*, 693 – emphasis added.
[50] Blaise Pascal, *Œuvres Complètes*, ed. L. Lafuma (Paris: Seuil, 1963) 189b.
[51] Marx, *Outlines of the Critique of Political Economy*, 693. It's at this point that we depart from anything that might be called a Marxist reading of Marx's text – i.e. from any conception

Mon Semblable, Mon Père(version)

Insofar as humanism has always involved the philosophical construction of an artificial "man" (e.g., Blake's "human abstract" & Mary Shelley's Frankensteinian "monster"), its methods of reasoning have tended towards either a politico-metaphysics or a generic reflexive accountability of social actions. This is based upon the assumption that technological processes are primarily ideational processes whose forms reify humanity as both agent & object of an otherwise historical consciousness. Whether metaphysical or genetic, the system of humanism necessitates a method of accounting for the status of artifice & generalised technē in the assumption of the stereotype of "man." Such a techno-methodology has been articulated diversely in the work of Marx, Heidegger & others. It extends beyond the socalled man-machine dialectic to the emergence of the symbolic order as the *technological locus* of what is to be called The Human. Marx's analytic of the machine should not be read as an account of a *reduction* of The Human's lifeworld socalled to the procedural-world of mere technics (or technical artefacts). We should read it as an account of that generalised "alien power" inherent in the "system of man."[52] This is one way of understanding what Marx calls "the general productive forces of the social brain."[53] These forces render the "individual" what Merleau-Ponty has termed "the consciousness of the phantom limb."[54]

If the subject, here, is bound to the motility of a social body, this is to the extent that it is simultaneously bound to a self-defining "means of production" from which it is also, paradoxically, alienated. The subject describes a "ghosting" or "amputation in advance" of some *thing*, as Freud says, that *thinks*. Humanity thus acquires the dubious status of a technological "afterthought," a pseudo-machine that makes reason (i.e., agency *tout court*) stand in a relation of prior possibility. This possibility is contained in no *thing* & marked by a logic of the interval, of temporalisation, as the constative "transition which does not get thought." Such a "prior" possibility – in the temporalised relation of being & the unthought – is also the forethrow of a "consciousness" that is both illegitimate & in advance of itself, describing its own counter-filiation

---

of technology as *historical immanence* – towards a notion (provisionally formulated) of temporalisation as *technological imminence*.

[52] Cf. John von Neumann & Oskar Morgenstern, *Theory of Games & Economic Behaviour* (Princeton: Princeton University Press, 1944).
[53] Marx, *Outlines of the Critique of Political Economy*, 695.
[54] Merleau-Ponty, *Phenomenology of Perception*, 93.

& genealogy. Implied in the intervention of a technē "at the origin," the logic of a *phantom consciousness* marks a supersession in the model of Cartesian physiology. Merleau-Ponty describes it as "the juxtaposition of a *process* in itself & a *cogitation*."[55]

From mean-ends production (eidos-telos) to the contingency of a generalised event-state, this shift from paradigm to stereotype brings into view a synecdochic dimension that interoperates "cause" & "condition." In this way, the human stereotype becomes a *technological* possibility dependent (tautologically) upon "the technological developments that secure man's existence," as Mumford says. However, the apparent inversion of the instrumentalist view of technology is not affected "dialectically" or through a transformation of the "human condition" by the advent of "mechanical reproduction," to borrow Walter Benjamin's phrase. It's a consequence of the disclosure, as Heidegger says, of what is most challenging in technology: humanity's confrontation with being. The confrontation takes place in a technological fantasy-society of designated monsters called the *proletariat*, which Benjamin alludes to as the *stuff* of an aestheticisation of politics wherein a nominal fascism changes place with the *essence of humanism* socalled.[56] Insofar as the particulate "human" designates a subjectivity, this can no longer be the inaugurating subjectivity of Cartesianism, nor the dialectical subjectivity of Hegelianism, nor the self-willed *a priori* subjectivity of Kant – but a subjectivity vested in technological agency, whose being is disclosed not by way of an act of the will, or of reason, but through the signifiability of its material interactions – as, for instance, in the operations of the Freudian unconscious, & ever more so in the development of cybernetics.[57]

Marx insists that, "What holds for machinery holds likewise for the combination of human activities & the development of human intercourse."[58] The system of mechanised interaction participates in the same stereotype of "social interaction," namely the interior interval of subjectivity. Moreover, it points to a "primordial" reflexivity underwriting the structural assumptions of intersubjectivity: the machine-processes described by Marx are predominantly autopoetic, *conscious linkages* that transform the purely mechanical into a generative

---

[55] Merleau-Ponty, *Phenomenology of Perception*, 102.
[56] See Walter Benjamin, "The Work of Art in the Age of Mechanical Reproduction," *Illuminations*, trans. Harry Zohn (London: Fontana, 1995).
[57] Cf. Norbert Wiener, *The Human Use of Human Beings: Cybernetics & Society* (Boston: Houghton Mifflin, 1950).
[58] Marx, *Outlines of the Critique of Political Economy*, 704-5.

technicity.[59] Merleau-Ponty identifies a comparable relation between a generalised motility & the twofold sense attributed to reflexivity, as "rational" agency & "unconscious" bodily operation. "The reflex," Merleau-Ponty argues, "does not arise from objective stimuli, but moves back towards them, & invests them with a meaning *which they do not possess* taken simply as psychological agents, but only when taken as a *situation*. It caused them to exist as a situation, it stands in a 'cognitive' relation to them, which means that it shows them up as that which it is destined to *confront*."[60]

Reflexivity thus defines the *id est* of a materiality not *already signified* but which *already signifies* – assuming, in effect, the position of an *ego cogito* of something *yet to be thought* & to which ("in other words") it thus refers (as both the figurative & literal horizon of "the unthought" & of "the unthinkable"). "It stands," Merleau-Ponty says, "in a 'cognitive' relation to them, which means that it shows them up as that which it is destined to *confront*."[61]

Heidegger (on whose account much of Merleau-Ponty's phenomenology devolves), argues that the essence of technology as Gestell or *en-framing*, "an ordering of destining, as is every way of revealing. Bringing-forth, *poiēsis*, is also a destining in this sense."[62] The analogy between poiēsis & Gestell points to how the challenge posed by technology reveals itself in the medialisation or *confrontation* of "Man" & "being." Elsewhere, in "The Principle of Identity" (1957), Heidegger defines Gestell as "the gathering of this challenge which places man & being face to face in such a way that they challenge each other" & affect a *critical disturbance* of the conventionalisation of *the human*. Consequently, Gestell is that "in which & from which man & being are of concern to each other in the technical world [...] In the mutual confrontation of man & being we discern the constellation of our age."[63] As a prelude to Ereignis or the technological "event," Gestell marks the way *technē* describes a relation to being that is one of "bringing-forth" (poiēsis) & of "revealing." In the *Nicomachean Ethics*, Aristotle says this category of possibility "is capable either of being or not being & [originates] in the

---

[59] See Mumford, *The Condition of Man*, 333.
[60] Merleau-Ponty, *Phenomenology of Perception*, 92 – emphasis added.
[61] Heidegger, "The Question Concerning Technology," 330.
[62] Martin Heidegger, *Identity & Difference*, trans. Joan Stambaugh (New York: Harper & Row, 1969 [1957]) 35.
[63] Aristotle, *Ethica Nicomachea* VI.4.1140a, trans. W.D. Ross, *The Works of Aristotle*, vol. IX (London: Oxford University Press, 1915).

maker & not in the thing made; for art [technē] is concerned neither with things that are, or come into being by necessity").[64]

Heidegger links the discursivity of *technē* to a concept of *readiness*, *disposability*, or *preparedness* (Bestand). He deploys a techno-logistal syntax to underwrite a condition of "the possible" whereby humanity's "own-most potential for being" is bound up with a procedural technicity. The translational *agent* of its bringing-forth (the "maker") is likewise bound up with the "machine" that "produces it & archives it"[65] in terms of the objectless potentiality in the Marxist structural relation of "fixed capital" to "surplus value." The matrix of Gestell-technē-poiēsis in Heidegger's analytic of technics, being & time is increasingly inflected by Marx's conception of temporality (i.e., *discursive communication*) among agents. Accordingly, agency concedes to a *signifying materiality* connected to a Heideggerian "indifferent subsistence" of difference[66] (e.g., a *ratio* between socalled fixed capital & the revenance-effect of technical reproduction). It's in this sense that Bestand needs to be understood as a temporalisation *without reserve* (i.e., production as entropy).[67] At a certain moment in Heidegger's text, Gestell comes to signify an "'event' of an opening in completion" through the "reciprocal 'need' of enframing & its other"; this "'appropriation' […] joins together the totalising drive of technology to the thinking that would exceed it."[68] All of this, then, is subsumed into the meaning of Ereignis.

---

[64] Jacques Derrida, "Typewriter Ribbon: Limited Ink (2) ('within such limits')," trans. Peggy Kamuf, *Material Events: Paul de Man & the Afterlife of Theory*, eds. Tom Cohen, Barbara Cohen, J. Hillis Miller & Andrzej Warminski (Minneapolis: University of Minnesota Press, 2001) 316.

[65] Heidegger, *Being & Time*, 430. This does not mean, however, that we should consider Heidegger as continuing, in any straightforward way, the work of Marx, as François Châtelet argues. Nor does it mean the contrary – as exemplified in the claim that Heidegger's early thinking was substantially directed *against* "the marxist conception of *alienation* (Entfremdung)," as Pierre Bourdieu argues. Bourdieu's reference to Heidegger's "Letter on Humanism," taken as an example of Heidegger's rejection of Marx, does not take account of the context in which the "Letter" was composed as an indirect response to Sartre's *Existentialism is a Humanism* (1946). Cf. Bourdieu, *The Political Ontology of Martin Heidegger*, trans. Peter Collier (Cambridge: Polity Press, 1991 [1988]) 94-5.

[66] On the "economy without reserve," cf. Georges Bataille, *La Part maudite* (Paris: Minuit, 1967).

[67] Translator's Forward to Heidegger, *Four Seminars*, xii.

[68] Heidegger, *Being & Time*, 437.

Technopoetics, or, Reason's "Other"

In the relation of technology to the "unthought" (or temporalisation) where humanity's being *exceeds* the thinkable, the question that emerges (& that Heidegger formulates most succinctly at the end of *Being & Time*) is: "Is there a way which leads from *primordial time* to the *meaning of being*? Does time itself manifest as the horizon of being?"[69] Between temporalisation as the unthought condition of technicity & the excess of thought that characterises the *time of being* as appropriation (Bestand), the "question concerning technology" is re-orientated according to a certain *unreasonable demand*, as Heidegger puts it. Hence: "The revealing that rules in modern technology is a challenging [Herausforden], which puts to nature the unreasonable demand that it supply energy which can be extracted & stored as such."[70]

This notion of surplus, echoing the abstract (symbolic) temporalisation of labour in Marx, thereby exceeds (or rather *détournes*) the rationale of productivity (as prolific nature), fixed in the present, upon which the Hegelian conception of primordiality (the initially pure unity of the self) is founded. There emerges a freedom of an "unrestricted self-equality"[71] that exposes a contradiction at the level of the "essence" of being as perpetual *becoming*. This contradiction has been widely discussed in terms of mechanical *reflexivity* & the interval of temporalisation implied by the logic of self-equality (being, of necessity, a logic of medialisation, of contiguity & recursivity). The notion of time, a primordial continuum, acquires the status of an unthought "in excess of itself," instantiated not in the metaphor of the Hegelian "pure concept" or "truth of consciousness" (Ichheit, egoity) – which, according to Heidegger, exists "solely in order [...] *not* to be a difference"[72] – but as a synecdoche of this excessive movement "itself." It is a temporalisation or recursion (the "*singularity & generality* of every 'I,'" as Derrida writes) within the structure of reflexivity. In addition to *readiness*, *disposability*, or *preparedness*, Heidegger calls this synecdoche an "expediting" & a "standing-reserve" (Bestand). Stiegler describes it as "access to anticipation" & its equivocation as "access to the possible."[73]

---

[69] Heidegger, "The Question Concerning Technology," 320.
[70] Heidegger, *Being & Time*, 433-4.
[71] Martin Heidegger, *Hegel's Phenomenology of Spirit*, trans. Parvis Emad & Kenneth Maly (Indianapolis: Indiana University Press, 1988) 125 – this volume constituting the lecture course given by Heidegger at the University of Freiburg, winter semester 1930-1.
[72] Stiegler, *Technics & Time*, 160.
[73] Marx, *Outlines of the Critique of Political Economy*, 707 – emphasis added.

In the Marxian ontology of the technological subject, "capital itself" is this "moving contradiction." Accordingly, technology (a "bringing-forth") represents a "becoming" bound to supersession as *accretive contiguity* & to the possibility of "instantiation" by way of deviation, redundancy & anachronism. The socalled essence of the human inflects this contradictory movement of a capital that "presses to reduce labour time to a minimum, while it posits labour time, on the other side, as the sole measure & source of wealth." Wealth (value) is here no longer bound to the idea of necessity (e.g., to the authentic determination of selfhood or the immanence of reason as freedom-of-the-will). It's bound to the arbitrary determinations of symbolic exchange & mechanical agency. In proportion to the degree that it "diminishes labour time in the necessary form so as to increase it in the superfluous form," capital (here designating the very *system* of value) "*posits the superfluous in growing measure as a condition* [...] *for the necessary*."[74]

In defining the individual's technological condition as one of supersession in which the figure of "man" operates neither as paradigm nor telos, but as a matrix or syntax of possibilities *articulated* via a recursive "temporalisation," the synecdochic character of standing reserve generalises the individual's status as *formal* & *textual*, binding it to the procedural substitutability & iterability of a general signifying system. The figure of the individual is temporalised insofar as it is tied to the *time of signification*. In Marx's schema, this mode of temporalisation figures in the trope of "the machine" – "systemic in its performance," Paul de Man says, "but arbitrary in its principle, like a grammar."[75] It is the complementarity of the individual-universal or what Marx terms its *trans-formation*. "In this transformation," Marx argues, "it is neither the direct human labour [the individual] performs, nor the time during which he works," by which humanity's technological condition is properly disclosed, "but rather the *appropriation* of his own general productive power, his understanding of nature & his mastery over it by virtue of his presence *as a social body* – it is, in a word, the development of the social individual which appears as the great foundation stone of production."[76]

---

[74] Paul de Man, "Semiology & Rhetoric," *Allegories of Reading: Figural Language in Rousseau, Nietzsche, Rilke & Proust* (New Haven: Yale University Press, 1979) 298.

[75] Marx, *Outlines of the Critique of Political Economy*, 705-6 – emphasis added.

[76] G.W.F. Hegel, *Elements of the Philosophy of Right*, ed. Allen W. Wood, trans. H.B. Nisbet (Cambridge: Cambridge University Press, 1991) 275ff.

Such a matrix of production suggests a generalised constructional or syntactic system underwriting the "discourse of man" in which mastery is bound up with a counter-movement of appropriation. It implies that its systematicity (i.e., its mechanism) is that of dynamic paradox rather than, for instance, "dialectical" homoeostasis. In any case, the mastery vested in this human hypothesis, as Marx presents it, is bound not to the exercise of individuated will, but to humanity's "presence as a social body." The figure of the individual operates synecdochically, & the "technological turn" of humanism does not resolve the paradox of technological agency. The turn devolves upon the paradox vis-à-vis the trope of what Marx calls the "social brain."

Secret Agent

The figuring of the human hypothesis as a technological event-state poses a challenge to the notion of the socius (& of the state as "ethical idea & objective freedom" vis-à-vis the *rational* constitution & corollary notion of the state *as individual*) found in Hegel's *Grundlinien der Philosophie des Rechts* (1821).[77] Dewey says this notion is founded upon "the realisation of *will*" as "the end of all institutions" wherein private ownership becomes "the expression of mastery of personality over physical nature [&] is a necessary element in such realisation."[78] The relationship of appropriation, property, mastery & will cannot, as Dewey notes, be dissolved here in a simple movement of dialectical overcoming in the idea of a "universal meaning that covers & dominates all particulars."[79] Instead, the synecdochic relation of the socius & individual articulated by way of an irreducible temporalisation ties the logic of appropriation to the recursive forethrow of an agency that is properly technological. In this schema, man is "the juxtaposition of a process in itself & a *cogitation*."

It is necessary to distinguish in Marx those lineaments of technological agency that pose "conscious linkage" not so much in opposition to the Hegelian concept of will, or even to the idea of calculated "self-interest," but as its détournement. Such "interests," Dewey remarks, "can be employed as vital terms only when the self is seen to be in process, & interest to be a name

---

[77] Dewey, *Reconstruction in Philosophy*, 189.
[78] Dewey, *Reconstruction in Philosophy*, 189.
[79] Dewey, *Reconstruction in Philosophy*, 195.

for whatever is concerned with furthering its movement."[80] What is called the "self" should be considered as a dynamic matrix of "conscious linkage" within the locus of a technological agency (Marx's "social brain"). We might say that agency is *conceded* vis-à-vis the assumption of a "metaphor" of collective consciousness in the operation of signs or circulation of value (i.e., symbolic exchange) accompanying the transductive relation of labour-time, surplus value, & the abstraction of the human stereotype (i.e., synecdoche or *characteristica generalis*). The logic of surplus affects a "temporal" movement of supersession & metonymic recursion that is "characterised," in Wiener's formulation, "by an invariance with respect to a shift of origin in time."[81] This denotes a tropological "equivalence across contiguity," which is the locus of what emerges in the figure of the human as quasi-individuated *subject*. Mediated by way of cybernetics, pragmatism & Marx, Heidegger's thinking of technology appears to culminate, Andrew Mitchell contends, "in a logic of replaceability (Ersetzbrakeit) & consumption (Verbrauch)."[81] This logic is summarised in the Heideggerian dictum: "Being is being-replaceable."[82]

The recursion of the temporal situates the human in relation to the "anticipation" of what Heidegger terms "an ordering of destining" (i.e., futurity) whereby what is held in reserve operates, complementarily, as a forethrow (e.g., of "potentiated" force, or power, in the sense of δύναμις; dynamism). This complementary movement is not teleological. It is an *accession* to the objectless occurrence of the "pure event" of possibility (viz., δύνασθαι, *to be able*). Insofar as the status of the human is bound to the trope of futurity as one whose being is revealed only by way of a challenge posed to the *idea* of what (human) being entails, technology must finally be regarded as no mere instrument of supersession or reification (i.e., of a technological *paradigm of man* or scientia generalis), but rather the collectively disclosed situation of the individual as a "mirror of anticipation."[83]

For Heidegger, then, the instrumental definition *necessarily* does not show us technology's essence. Nor does it provide grounds for an assumption of autonomous agency in man's relationship to socalled

---

[80] Norbert Wiener, *Cybernetics; or, Control & Communication in the Animal & the Machine* (Cambridge, Mass.: MIT Press, 1965 [1948]) viii-ix.

[81] Translator's Forward to Martin Heidegger, *Four Seminars*, trans. Andrew Mitchell & François Raffoul (Bloomington: Indiana University Press, 2003) xi.

[82] Heidegger, *Four Seminars*, 62.

[83] Stiegler, *Technics & Time*, 153.

technical objects. In clear contrast to Hegel's definition of the machine as an autonomous tool, Heidegger argues: "Seen in terms of the standing-reserve, the machine is completely non-autonomous, for it has its standing only on the basis of the ordering of the orderable."[84] "The machine" is not the mere abstraction of labour, divided off from the human stereotype & operating in its stead. It is the inscription of humanity's horizon of being & antecedent condition within the appearance of orderability (i.e., by way of a certain *calculus of the possible*). This particular inflexion of the Marxian concept of time & value has often been interpreted as providing the epistemological (& onto-anthropological) criteria for a type of cyber-humanism, according to which "technology" constitutes a "cultural system that reconstructs the entire social world as an object of control."[85]

Control, in this context, is an emergent structure of organisation "programmed" by material constraint or probability. Consequently, as Herbert Marcuse has claimed (although for different reasons), "technological rationality has become political rationality,"[86] insofar as politics describes an "architectonic" science devolving not upon an "instrumental maieutics" or "technological mastery" of prevailing conditions in the lifeworld, but upon what Stiegler calls "the material trace of the stereotype."[87] (That is to say, upon the typological criteria defined by a mechanics of variable probabilities – e.g., in a disclosure of being "from time into time," as Heidegger says – thus defining the "operative role" of the humanistic stereotype.) This leads Heidegger to the following question: "What is the instrumental itself?" And this question leads him to an analysis of the relationship between instrument & cause & of fourfold causality (causa materialis; causa formalis; causa finalis; causa efficiens). The status of cause (i.e., "that which brings about") *occasions* (re the Aristotelian conception of *aition*, "that to which something is *indebted*")[88] the relation of eidos, telos, logos & what Hegel terms primordiality & what Stiegler elsewhere terms the "memory of the stereotype" (i.e., the techno-mimetics of "consciousness"[89] as pre-presentation of causes). Causal-instrumentality is thereby re-conceived in terms of a reflexivity that, by consequence,

---

[84] Heidegger, "The Question Concerning Technology," 322-3.

[85] Andrew Feenberg, *Transforming Technology: A Critical Theory Revisited* (Oxford: Oxford University Press, 2002) 6-7.

[86] Herbert Marcuse, *One Dimensional Man: Studies in the Ideology of Advanced Industrial Society* (Boston: Becon Press, 1964) xv-xvi.

[87] Stiegler, *Technics & Time*, 158.

[88] Heidegger, "The Question Concerning Technology," 314 – emphasis added.

[89] Stiegler, *Technics & Time*, 151.

delineates a subject as generalised temporalisation: the virtuality of an event *in advance of itself*, underwriting all the "economies of thought" or, for example, the "motivating factors" of any sign operation tending to what is called symbolic exchange or the circulation of value, & so on. This would also describe what Derrida calls "the differential deployment of *technē*, of techno-science or teletechnology,"[90] as the *spatialising of temporality* (i.e., as a movement of metonymic contiguity (partes extra partes) & synecdochic equivalence, which Derrida elsewhere designates by *différance*).

A Very Moving Contradiction

If the entropement of causal ambivalence characteristic of technē as *temporalisation* (différance) reveals, Heidegger argues, "whatever does not bring itself forth & does not yet lie here before us, whatever can look & turn out now one way & now another,"[91] this is principally because it marks a *heterotechnical* relation of eidos-telos-logos. This ambivalence is not merely the ambivalence of efficient causes. It defines what, in place of any a priori system of a *state of affairs* – of an *initial state* or of a *primordiality* – conditions the indeterminacy of "the event" as technological & thereby instigative "in the first place" of a system. In the socio-technical problematic outlined by Marx, this event-state ambivalence points to "something constitutionally heterogeneous to the social system or structure," according to Ernesto Laclau (channelling de Man), which is "present in the latter from the very beginning, preventing it from constituting itself as a closed or representable reality."[92]

Yet here, again, the assumption of such a closure or "representability of the real" interjects itself as the *real* spectre of dialectics – not the totalising movement that, by rhetorical sleight of hand, encloses the real in the symbolic, but the originary difference that gives the imaginary *in place of it* (i.e., in place of the "it" to which the *idea of the real* supposedly corresponds, whether it be "representable" or not). Hence Freud's remarks apropos of the Id & (its objectified *imminence* in) the Ego: "wo es war, soll Ich werden" Subjectivity gravitates towards this "it" as though under a wordless, unsymboliseable

---

[90] Jacques Derrida, *Specters of Marx: The State of the Debt, the Work of Mourning, & the New International*, trans. Peggy Kamuf (London: Routledge, 1994) 169.

[91] Heidegger, "The Question Concerning Technology," 319.

[92] Ernesto Laclau, "The Politics of Rhetoric," *Material Events: Paul de Man & the Afterlife of Theory*, eds. Tom Cohen, Barbara Cohen, J. Hillis Miller & Andrzej Warminski (Minneapolis: University of Minnesota Press, 2001) 230.

compulsion of which the Ego is nevertheless the signifier *par excellence*, since it is the object-automatism of the Ego, & not any subjectivity, that comes to *think* & to perform what Marx calls the "conscious linkages" of the symbolic mechanism (i.e., of socalled representation). This is a long way from the implied *immanence* of closure or representability of a real that is merely impeded by the heterogeneity of its constituting event, or the indeterminacy of its outcomes ("now one way & now another").

Considered both as "totalisation" & "particularisation" (metonymy, synecdoche), this machinic Ego indicates a general relation of singularity to the status of the in-dividual as *figure* of the event-state – i.e., in accordance with what de Man describes firstly as a "pattern of substitution that all tropes have in common," & secondly as "the difference necessarily introduced by substitution"[93] – *introduced* in the sense of an interval of spatio-temporalisation. Not implied immanence – even of the unrepresentable – but situationality is what, for de Man, defines the Ego as "*heterogeneous with regard to the system*."[94] In addition, this heterogeneity describes a "generalised system" of "metonymic displacements articulated by relations of contiguity,"[95] exemplified above all for de Man by a synecdoche: "The synecdoche that substitutes part for whole & whole for part [&] is in fact a metaphor, powerful enough to transform temporal contiguity into an infinite duration."[96]

What does such a transformation mean, if not a certain paradox of equivalence ("infinite duration") delineated within a system of evolutionary discontinuity or morphogenesis? That is to say, *within* the very interval of technopoetic recursion, wherein the forethrow of temporalisation demarcates "what endures" as nothing other than the recursive moment? In speaking of the transduction of contiguity into infinite duration (as de Man does), there is necessarily implied what Derrida frequently refers to as *prosthesis of/at the origin*.[97] This double movement, at the limits of ordinality, of equivalence & contiguity is the stereotypical movement par excellence. And it is in accordance with this double logic of the stereotype that the machine (as the "figure" of a generalised technology) discloses a being-as-event-of-the-unthought,

---

[93] Paul de Man, *Aesthetic Ideology*, ed. Andrzej Warminski (Minneapolis: University of Minnesota Press, 1996) 62-3.

[94] de Man, *Aesthetic Ideology*, 59.

[95] Laclau, "The Politics of Rhetoric," 237.

[96] de Man, *Aesthetic Ideology*, 63.

[97] As heterotechnical, or hetero-temporal, relation of primordiality to an emplacement-in-advance.

of the *excess* of thought, of futurity, temporalisation, technological imminence – of the spectre of an impending *to-come* that simultaneously holds itself in reserve: the impossible.

L'humanité n'existe pas

Contrary to the belief it comprises an aggregate-of-reason, the fundamental *ambivalence* of the human stereotype brings into view a *rationalisation after the event*. The sense in which technology "represents the completion of the logic governing metaphysics & *to that extent*" is "likewise an opening" ought to indicate that the dynamic interval of an "originary technicity" cannot simply be negativised – e.g., as *preventative* of a system (i.e., of "human artefacts") constituting itself – as though it were nothing other than a type of prophylactic. Nor can it be negativised as the withholding of some *thing* – of some essential expenditure or consumption – an in-completion in effect that interrupts only insofar as it is circumscribable (& therefore can always be transcended by one means or another). Instead, this "event of an opening," of an immeasurable possibility, discloses the inception or *inter-ception* of an Ego only as that lability which "joins the totalising drive of technology to the thinking that would exceed it"[98] (i.e., as synechdoche or metonymic recursion, according to which surplus value "*ceases to be localisable*"[99] in the figure of an *individual* not already traversed by the movement of ambivalence).

"Here we can see once again," to interpolate from Hardt & Negri's remarks on the state of economic globalisation, "the importance of the revolution of Renaissance humanism. *Ni Dieu, ni maître, ni l'homme* – no transcendent power or measure will determine the values of our world. Value will be determined only by *humanity's own continuous innovation & creation*."[100] The challenge posed to the sheer inertia of humanism by the Marxian "machine" is none other than the subversion of the human as *emancipated consciousness* by situating it, not as a locus of circulatory value, but as what is most problematic in the structure & relation of value (of the teleology of meaning; as the stereotype of the *idea-to-come*, against

---

[98] Forward to Heidegger, *Four Seminars*, xii.
[99] Gilles Deleuze & Félix Guattari, *A Thousand Plateaus: Capitalism & Schizophrenia*, trans. Brian Massumi (Minneapolis: University of Minnesota Press, 1993) 491.
[100] Michael Hardt & Antonio Negri, *Empire* (Cambridge, Mass.: Harvard University Press, 2000) 356 – emphasis added.

which is posed the very trope of *anticipation*). A remark by Deleuze provides an interesting dilation on this theme:

> The famous phrase of the *Contribution to the Critique of Political Economy*, "mankind always sets itself only such tasks as it can solve," does not mean that the problems are only apparent or that they are already solved, but, on the contrary, that the economic conditions of a problem determine or give rise to the manner in which it finds a solution within the framework of the real relations of the society. Not that the observer can draw the least optimism from this, for these "solutions" may involve stupidity or cruelty, the horror of war or the "solution of the Jewish problem." More precisely, the solution is always that which a society deserves or gives rise to as a consequence of the manner in which, given its real relations, it is able to pose the problems set within it & to it by the differential relations it incarnates.[101]

In the *assumption of a problem as such* – in the *paradigm* of the problem, made manifest under conditions of an economimēsis (to which "society," its "real relations," "man," are posed as the necessary *correlative*) – we are finally confronting the status of the technological within the discourse of humanism. In short, technology will have acquired the status of that which is most *problematic*, insofar as "technology" is characterised by the repetition & deferral of its object ("humanity") onto the general category of the unthought, the in-excess-of-itself, the immeasurable, & hence of an open possibility. This is because technology can't be reduced to a "problem" humanity sets itself. And if technology assumes the complexion & complexity of such a problem, for which humanity (increasingly a synonym for the very *agency of capital* by which it is "alienated") is the anticipated solution, this is because it represents that ideal self-supersession by means of which humanity nevertheless imagines it can *live on*, as prosthesis of a prosthesis. Precisely for the same reason, in assuming the character of a reflexivity still bound to the rhetoric of a science of reasoned cause (of a problematic as such), this post-human becomes, if not an *instrumentum*, a *matière instrumentale*.

Humanity is thus neither transcended nor contradicted by the machine, but instead is "produced by the very possibility of the machine." That is, by "the machine-like expropriation" by which the socalled essence of humanity's being-for-itself (as *division-of-labour*) is encountered by way of "technicity, programming, repetition, or iterability."[102] And insofar as

---

[101] Deleuze, *Difference & Repetition*, 186.
[102] Derrida, "Typewriter Ribbon," 335; 336.

the machine describes the fundamental modus operandi of what Marx calls productive capital – as this "moving contradiction" – technology is thus "no mere means" nor even, as Heidegger would have it, an "enframing" & "a way of revealing."[103] Yet as the autopoiēsis of surplus or "standing reserve," the immeasurability of the machine describes a compulsively entropic movement from the post-production of the human stereotype to the reification of its end: not as an essence revealed in the pure ontology of its being (as plenitude of self-evidence), but as the very contrary, the sign of its "ownmost" impossibility.

---

[103] Heidegger, "The Question Concerning Technology," 318.

www.ingramcontent.com/pod-product-compliance
Lightning Source LLC
Chambersburg PA
CBHW032055090426
42744CB00005B/229